THE BOATING EMERGENCY MANUAL

Also by Tony Meisel

The Rule of St. Benedict
American Wine
A Manual of Singlehanded Sailing
Under Sail
Singlehanding: A Sailor's Guide
Yachting: A Turn-of-the-Century Treasury
The Boat Maintenance and Repair Book

THE BOATING EMERGENCY

MANUAL

Sail & Power

TONY MEISEL

COLLIER BOOKS
Macmillan Publishing Company
New York
Collier Macmillan Publishers
London

Collier Books
Macmillan Publishing Company
866 Third Avenue, New York, NY 10022
Collier Macmillan Canada, Inc.

Library of Congress Cataloging-in-Publication Data
Meisel, Tony.
   The boating emergency manual/Tony Meisel
      p.   cm.
   Includes index.
   ISBN 0-02-044481-8
   1. Boats and boating–Safety measures–Handbooks, manuals, etc.
I. Title.
VK200.M35 1989
623.88'8–dc19   88-8512
                                    CIP

Macmillan books are available at special discounts for bulk purchases for sales promotions, premiums, fund-raising or educational use. For details, contact:

Special Sales Director
Macmillan Publishing Company
866 Third Avenue
New York, NY 10022

This book has been designed and typeset by the author on a Macintosh Plus computer and an Apple LaserWriter Plus printer using MicroSoft Word and Aldus PageMaker software. The typeface is Adobe Postscript Souvenir.

10 9 8 7 6 5 4 3 2 1

Printed in the United States of America

CONTENTS

INTRODUCTION

When something goes wrong at sea, it is invariably a problem you have never before experienced, the weather conditions are worsening and time is of the essence. You are unsure of the best course of action, and you cannot afford to spend precious time searching for the precise answer to your actual dilemma. All your accumulated knowledge from books, previous experience, casual talk and regimented study suddenly seems too distant, too technical.

You need to think on your feet. Assuming you can retain your wits in the face of the unknown or the spectre of disaster, basic information can be adjusted and reinterpreted to fit a particular situation. This book is designed to both supply the basics and give you the mental framework for solving your problem yourself.

Herein you will find direct responses to a number of nautical emergency situations. Other actions will be possible. More permanent repairs may be needed later. The state of sea and wind may force modifications in the advice. But you will have some sort of ready reference, and answer to a tightening throat and rising fear, to the question, *What now?*

Obviously, no one volume could cover every possible contingency. Every yacht and yachtsman is different and each has capabilities unknown to this author. The assumption throughout is that you know your boat and its abilities and, hopefully, you know your own as well. Don't overestimate your knowledge and skills. Ego is deadly on the water.

No known substitute exists for experience and the knowledge acquired through errors and mistakes rectified. In an emergency, the initial response is usually panic. Repress it! Panic is wonderful for the climax in a disaster movie. It has no place aboard any vessel. Remember the *Titanic*? To be a proficient seaman, you must learn to think everything through, to gauge speed and distance, to know wind speed from the look of the water's surface, to be able to judge the inertial movement of your hull in different types of weather.

Safe and enjoyable boating is the result of applied knowledge, and that comes from practice, practice and more practice. This book will give you responses in a general way to most emergency situations. But your accumulated knowledge and experience is what will allow you to adapt the advice and procedures described herein to the particular situation *you* have to face.

Good boating!

Tony Meisel
New Suffolk, NY

ABANDONING SHIP

❶ PREPARE LIFE RAFT OR DINGHY... BUT ONLY IF THE SHIP IS FOUNDERING.

❷ GATHER UP NECESSARY EXTRA EMERGENCY GEAR AND IMPORTANT PAPERS.

❸ REMAIN FULLY CLOTHED.

❹ BE PREPARED TO CUT TETHER ONLY AFTER ALL CREW IS ABOARD LIFE RAFT.

❺ TAKE PROPER PRECAUTIONS IF USING A DINGHY WHEN NO LIFE RAFT IS AVAILABLE.

❻ IF NO LIFE RAFT, WEAR LIFE JACKET AND ENTER WATER FROM WINDWARD SIDE.

❼ IF PICKED UP BY SHIP OR HELICOPTER, SEE BELOW.

1. If, and only if, the mother ship is in imminent danger of sinking, inflate life raft on deck or by tossing overboard to activate CO_2 cylinders. Do not attempt to right the raft until necessary.

2. Extra water, food, etc., should be packed at hand in a duffle. Tie it to the raft if possible. Ship's papers, passports, etc., should be in a waterproof pouch, responsibility of the captain. If at all possible, get extra flares, radio emergency beacon and a compass aboard, as well as chart of the area. All this takes preplanning.

3. Hypothermia is one of the surest ways to quick death. Keep fully clothed, including hat and boots. Water within the oilskins will have something of a wetsuit effect, and the wet clothing, especially if wool, will have a high insulating effect. Move as little as possible, only so much as is necessary to stay afloat. Attempting to swim, no matter how strong a swimmer you are, will result in heat loss on a massive scale, unconsciousness and death.

4. Leave the raft tethered to the ship. Too many people have been lost attempting to leap from ship to raft. Only when every member of the crew is aboard should the tether be cut. Take what care you can not to cut the raft also.

Be especially careful when inflating the life raft that it does not catch up on rigging or cockpit controls. Once inflated, it will be very difficult to dislodge and damage is possible.

All rafts come packed with some survival equipment. Be sure extra supplies are at hand, especially water.

5. A dinghy can be used if the life raft is not functioning or if there is none. It should be fitted out before hand, especially with a strong and sufficient size sea anchor to hold it bow to wind. However, since no dinghy (or virtually none) is designed for life-raft use, certain precautions are necessary. First, a rigid boat will need to be heavily fendered to avoid damage from the mother ship. Second, boarding will be extremely difficult and dangerous in anything approaching heavy seas. Third, an enclosed form of protection–canopies, dodger, etc.–will be necessary to avoid boarding seas and exposure. Fourth, permanent flotation is an absolute need. To board a dinghy, be sure to coordinate your stepping aboard with the rhythm of the two boats; otherwise you may step into thin air and descend rapidly to break limbs upon your sudden entry. Do not untether from the yacht until all members of the crew have boarded.

6. If no life raft or dinghy exists, put on your life jacket, and enter the water from the windward side of the boat. From any other point the boat can drift down, or back down or slip to windward, endangering anyone in the water. Keep all clothes on, and assume a fetal position to conserve body heat. A light, whistle and knife should be attached to the life vest. Try to stay calm.

7. Pickup by ship or helicopter is a dangerous, touchy and frightening maneuver. Inevitably the ship will be larger than your vessel, and the chances of collision and dismasting are great, even in calm seas. You will be distraught and tired. Try to be hoisted aboard, rather than climb a ladder. Leave the yacht from bow or stern and time the move up to coincide with the crest of a wave. In heavy weather you will probably be safer in the lee of the larger ship, but you must move fast. Do *not* worry about your yacht! It can be replaced. Helicopter rescues demand even more thought on your part. Clear the cockpit and release any rigging located there, even if the mast goes over forward. Do *not*, repeat *do not*, fasten the helicopter line to any part of your vessel! Grab the harness lowered and, as quickly as possible, help each crew member into it. At each pass of the copter be prepared to snag that line. In heavy seas it will be difficult, in strong winds even more so. Signal green if prepared to leave, red if not. Another possibility and perhaps safer is to be picked up from the dinghy or life raft towed astern. However, this makes you a smaller target, and gives a less stable platform for the pickup.

Make sure the raft is upright, totally inflated and tethered before the first person attempts boarding.

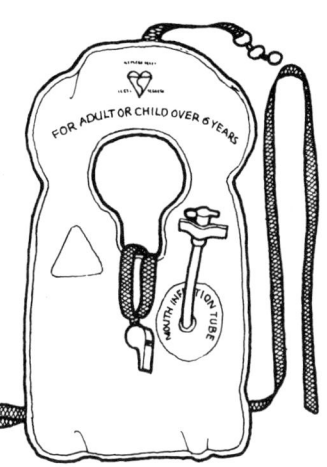

Life vests are an absolute must in heavy weather. Both foam-filled and CO_2 inflatable are suitable so long as they carry certification from government agencies.

Rigid dinghies can be used as life rafts if properly prepped. A sailing rig which stows within the craft can be a lifesaver, especially off the beaten track.

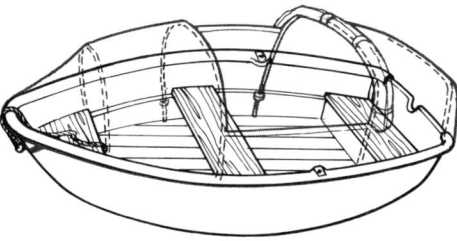

Boarding can be exceedingly dangerous. One person should be aboard and fending off before anyone else attempts entry. Keep the raft tethered to the mother ship until all are aboard.

If you end up in the water, try to assume a relaxed and natural position. This will not be easy. Concentration is necessary. Once the shock of entry has passed, use all your facilities to relax. Movement will only dissipate valuable body heat and exhaust you.

Helicopter or ship pickup is a dangerous job. Be prepared to follow directions from the 'copter or ship, as you will probably be too tired and frightened to think clearly.

AGROUND

❶ DETERMINE WIND DIRECTION.

❷ DETERMINE STATE OF TIDE.

❸ IN OFFSHORE WIND, BACK SAILS.

❹ IN ONSHORE WIND, DROP SAILS, APPLY REVERSE ENGINE GENTLY.

❺ ON RISING TIDE, FOLLOW ABOVE.

❻ ON FALLING TIDE, ROW KEDGE ANCHOR AND WARP TO DEEPER WATER; SET KEDGE AND APPLY WARP TO WINCH, OR WITH BRIDLE TO TWO WINCHES.

1. Backing sails can lead to accidental jibe. Be prepared. You may be better off dropping the jib and backing main. This will keep the foredeck clear for anchor handling.

2. Onshore winds can vary in strength, of course. In a gale the engine will probably not be sufficiently powerful to pull you off the ground. You will have to set a kedge. Do it carefully in heavy conditions. If you plan to kedge and power at the same time be wary of fouling the propeller with the kedge warp. Either keep it taut or use floating line.

3. If the tide is falling rapidly, best prepare to dry out as comfortably as possible. With fast ebb and heavy seas you may have to prepare to abandon ship, especially if the boat is on rocks.

4. If the tide is rising and you are on a lee shore, get the kedge out as fast as possible or you may be swept further ashore.

5. Much depends on the profile and configuration of the boat's keel. If a long, sloping keel, you will have less trouble backing off. If a fin keel, you may be able to spin the boat about and reach or run off into deeper water. Twin-keel boats should not be heeled, as you will only increase the draft. In calm conditions, prepare to sit out the tide. In heavy going, you will have to kedge or power off.

When backing sails in shifty conditions be prepared to drop sail quickly, and be prepared for accidental jibes. In strong winds, use the foresail.

When setting a kedge, be careful to coil the rode loosely to avoid delay and wasted effort.

6. Heeling a single-keeled boat can be accomplished in several ways: move the crew to the shallow water deck; swing crew or loaded dinghy off the boom end. In a very small boat, you may be able to use the main halyard taken ashore for leverage. (Beware: masthead fittings cannot take much abuse. Do not try this maneuver in a heavy-displacement vessel.)

7. You may be able to reduce draft by lightening ship. Remove heavy gear to the dinghy, possibly drain water tanks. In a light displacement boat, this could decrease draft by the inch or two needed to free the keel.

8. Hauling off can be done with a bow anchor while the crew heels the boat. May also be accomplished by an aiding vessel. If another ship can help, first make sure that questions of salvage are resolved. Then, depending on your position, pass *your* line to the assisting vessel. First make the line secure to foredeck bollard or stern cleats with a bridle, or secure it around the mast or cabin house. Instruct the other vessel to slowly pull you seaward without any surge of acceleration. This is most important. A quick application of throttle could result in torn decks or dismasting. When you are free and able to maneuver, request your line freed. For such tows, polypropylene cordage, because it floats, is best employed, lessening the chances of fouled propellers and rudders.

Heeling a twin keel boat will only worsen the situation.

Using weights attached to a swung-out boom can help lift the keel.

Legs can be rigged in a drying-out situation provided you have a long and stout spar aboard. Lashings should be devised to allow easy release without having to dive (left).

Hauling or towing can damage the boat. Be sure to direct any towboat to move slowly, with no fast acceleration. Also make sure towropes are secured to minimize strain on deck gear.

ANCHORING

❶ DETERMINE THE STATE OF TIDE.

❷ DETERMINE THE BOTTOM COMPOSITION.

❸ LOWER THE ANCHOR OVER THE BOWS GENTLY.

❹ PAY OUT APPROPRIATE SCOPE.

❺ SNUB THE ANCHOR.

❻ MAKE FAST.

1. The state of the tide and rate of inflow and outflow is vital. In areas of small tidal range, such as the Mediterranean or the Chesapeake, this is not quite so important, but make sure you have allowed for low springs when assaying the position the boat will take when anchored. Allow for swinging room and for reversal of position when the tide changes. In areas of vast tidal range, with swift inrushing tides, such as Brittany or Newfoundland, where ranges can be upward of 30 feet, you will have to anchor far out with very long cables. In such conditions, two anchors should probably be set, especially when tides boil in at as much as 10 knots.

2. Bottom composition can be determined by depth sounder, chart reference or hand lead armed with tallow or grease. The bottom will determine the type and size of anchor you set. Mud, soft sand and mixed bottoms indicate a Danforth-type or plow anchor. Hard sand, as is found in the Aegean and Carribean, will hold with either but may demand hand setting. Weed will foil a Danforth with ease, and sometimes a plow. Rocky bottoms will be best served with a good old-fashioned fisherman (Herreshoff preferred–if you can find one) or a Bruce anchor. These two will usually dig past weed the best. If the bottom is mixed–small pebbles or shale, or weed and shale–use a fisherman; the goal will be to get underneath the top layer as quickly as possible. Coral accepts fishermen and plows best, though the shank of a plow can be badly bent by coral and chain cable is almost a necessity to avoid chafe. If it can be found, I have discovered the Northill anchor to be the most use over the widest range of conditions.

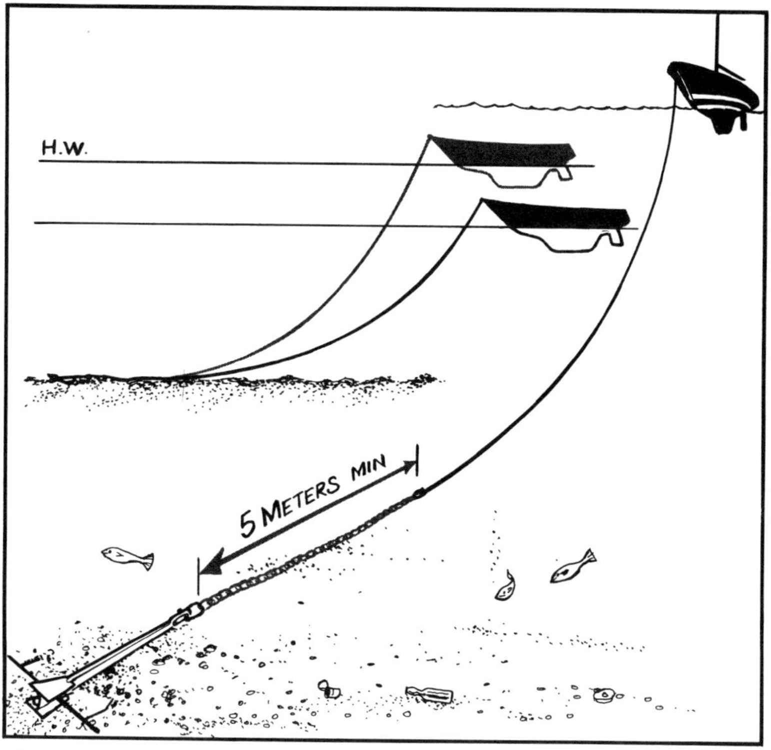

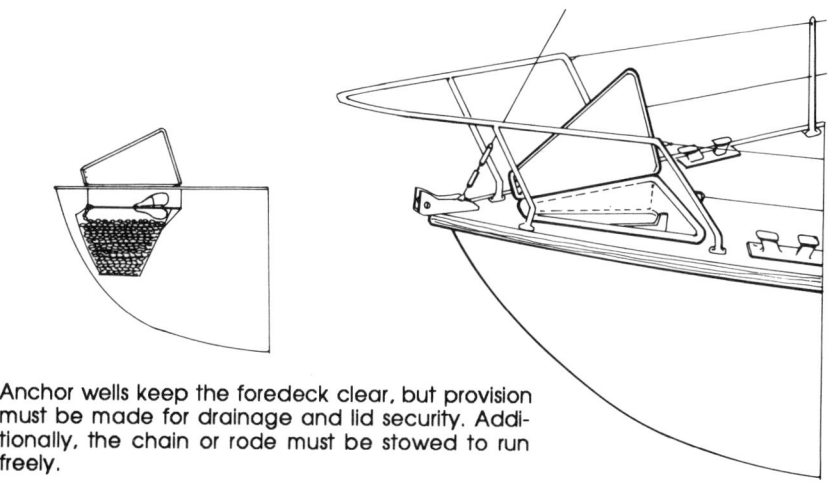

All anchors set to a fiber rode need at least 5 meters of heavy chain between anchor and rode to reduce chafe and to increase holding power.

Anchor wells keep the foredeck clear, but provision must be made for drainage and lid security. Additionally, the chain or rode must be stowed to run freely.

3. Too often anchors are tossed, dropped or slung over the bows. By carefully and slowly lowering it you will be able to ascertain the rate of drift, and will avoid permanently damaging the hull, deck or yourself.

4. Scope depends upon depth at high water, holding ground and whether chain or rope cable is used. All rope cables should have at least 5 meters of chain between the end of the rope and the anchor to prevent chafe and increase holding power. All chain permits shorter scope (as little as 3:1), but can snub more easily than rope. Rope, having great elasticity (nylon) will act as a better shock absorber, especially when in surging conditions. However, rope must be heavily padded–either with patent chafe gear or rags or leather–to avoid catastrophe at the stemhead, roller or chocks. The holding ground will make a difference; the better the bottom, the less the scope. Mud and soft sand will usually hold best, assuming the appropriate anchor. In any case, be prepared to set rope cable with a minimum of 6:1 scope and chain with a minimum of 4:1 scope. Under deteriorating weather and sea conditions, scope should be increased and the possibility of a second or even third anchor being set must be considered.

5. Making sure the anchor is set is the most important single step you can take in achoring. Either back the sails, throw the engine in reverse or hand snub it when the appropriate amount of scope has been payed out. Be sure the cable is attached to a strong point below decks and is secured to the samson post, cleat or anchor winch. Even with chain cable a nylon preventer is a good idea–especially as cables have an appalling tendency to snap at the stemhead fitting or roller. Rig the preventer from a second cleat inboard to the cable a couple of feet outboard of the stem. Not only can this save you an anchor and cable, but will act as a shock absorber in heavy surge situations.

6. Not only should the inboard end of the cable be securely fastened to the ship, but the cable must be bowsed down in the proper stemhead fitting. In a roller, the cheeks must be high enough to prevent the cable from jumping out; a retaining pin should be fitted, and all metal should be filed down so that no sharp edges are evident at any point at which the cable *might* touch the roller or cheeks. Chain can be weakened by friction against metal! If your roller lacks a retaining pin, or if you must pass the cable through a chock, use a short length of light stuff to tie down the rope or chain, either around the fitting or in some way to close off the openings and make for a rope loop.

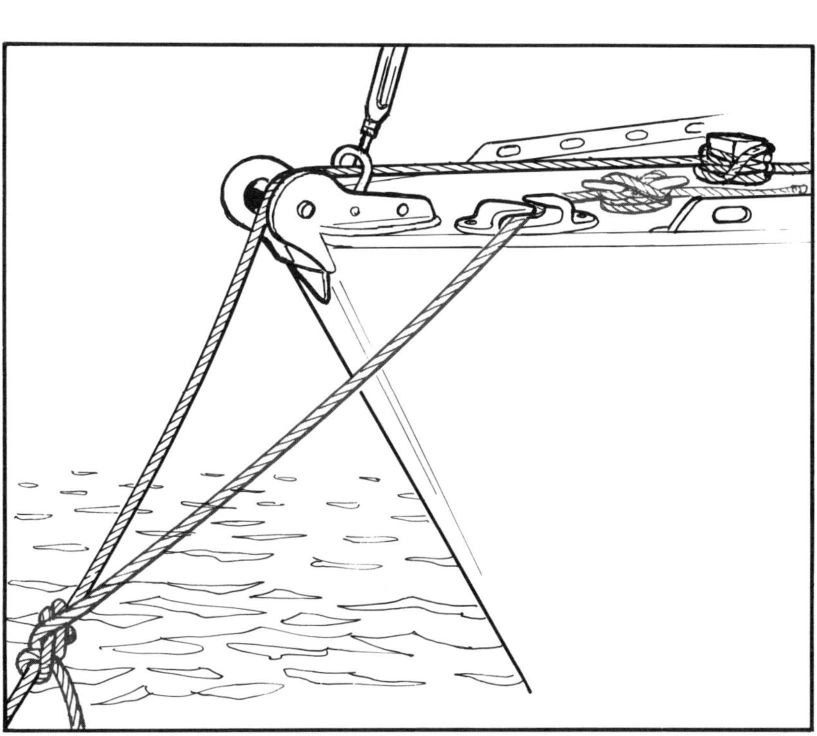

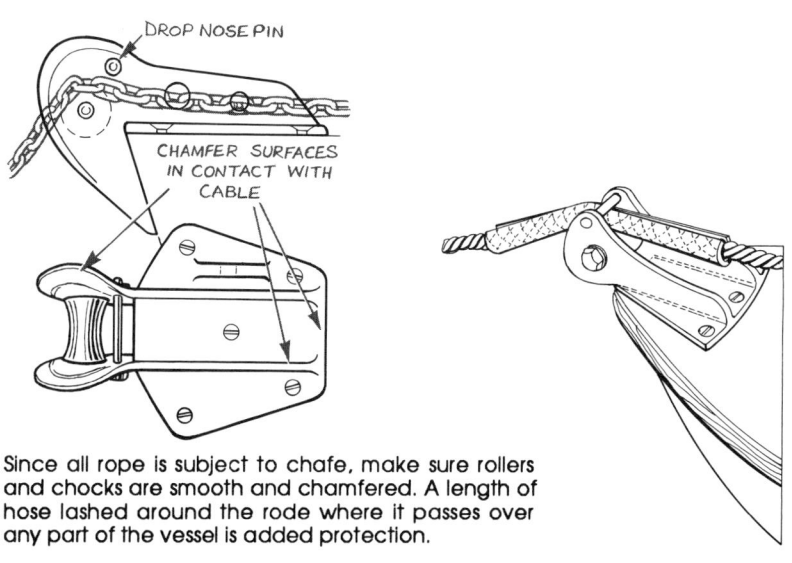

A nylon preventer will help ease strain on the anchor cable.

DROP NOSE PIN

CHAMFER SURFACES IN CONTACT WITH CABLE

Since all rope is subject to chafe, make sure rollers and chocks are smooth and chamfered. A length of hose lashed around the rode where it passes over any part of the vessel is added protection.

ANCHORING: *Special*

❶ CHANGING WIND DIRECTION DEMANDS A SECOND ANCHOR.

❷ TIDAL STREAM CHANGES MEAN FORE-AND-AFT ANCHOR-ING.

❸ ANCHORING IN HEAVY WEATHER CAN MEAN ANOTHER AN-CHOR AND A RIDING WEIGHT.

❹ DRAGGING CALLS FOR FAST EVASIVE ACTION.

❺ FOULING DEMANDS FORETHOUGHT.

❻ TRIP LINES.

❼ SHORT-HANDED ANCHORING TECHNIQUES.

1. When the wind shows signs of veering, be prepared to lay out a second anchor. The second anchor can be the kedge and can be equipped with chain and rope cable. Lower it off the bows in the direction from which the wind is veering. Pay out cable as the boat begins to swing until more or less equal strain is taken by both anchors and the boat becomes the fulcrum of an easy-swinging pendulum, so to speak.

2. In a river where the tidal stream runs strong and will reverse or where there is little or no room to swing, anchoring fore-and-aft is called for. Anchor in the normal way, letting out double the amount of cable needed for the situation—a good reason to carry at least 75 to 100 meters of cable—and set the hook. Then drop a stern anchor and motor or winch the ship forward, paying out cable to get the ship in the required position. Be sure to station someone in the bow to take in the excess cable at the same time you are moving forward, otherwise you chance fouling the propeller or wrapping a rope cable around the keel or skeg or rudder. Be sure to allow a small amount of slack at high water, in both cables, but not so much as to make for uncomfortable movement.

3. Anchoring in heavy weather or off a lee shore is always a fearful and difficult experience. However, there are times when no other alternative permits itself. Two basic methods are available for effective holding power. *First*, drop one anchor in the normal manner,

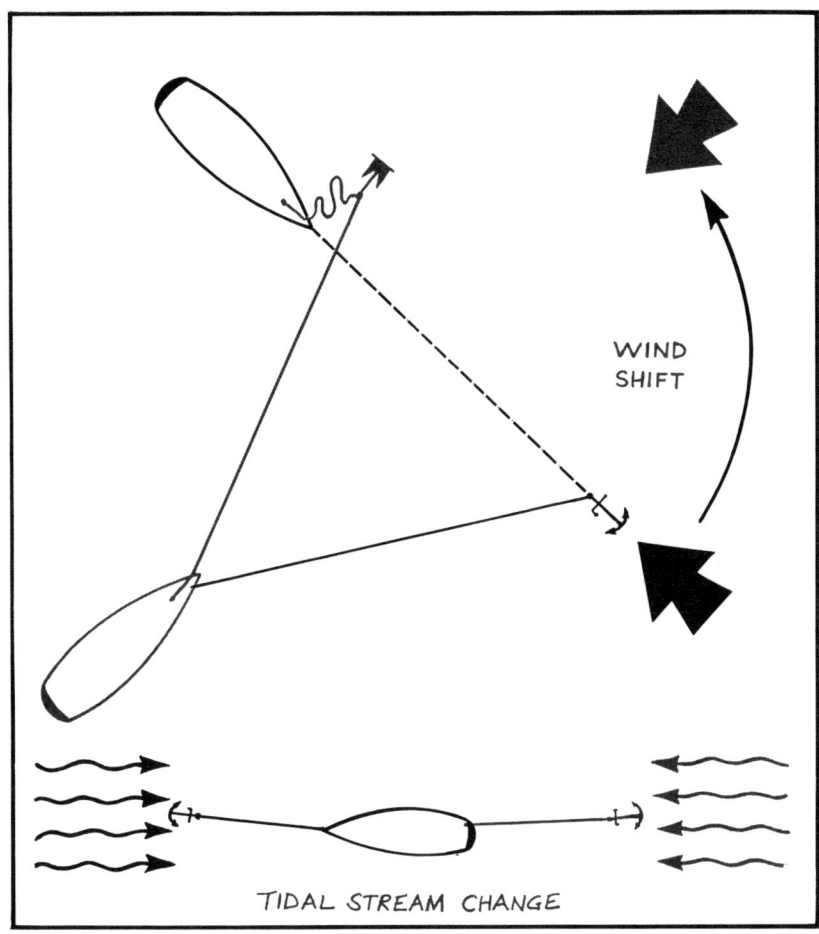

WIND SHIFT

TIDAL STREAM CHANGE

Laying out a second anchor, either at an angle or fore-and-aft, should be considered whenever there is a chance of wind shift or tidal change. Since strain will be greater on one than the other, both should be of size and weight consistent with the main anchor. In storm conditions, three anchors may be advisable, with the main one in line with the expected storm track, the other two to either side.

paying out double the length of cable needed. Then lay a second–much as fore-and-aft technique–bringing up on the first cable. If the two anchors are laid, one to windward and one to leeward, the chances of holding in a wind shift are greatly increased, especially important when anchoring not far offshore in an open roadstead. Lay out extra cable so that both lines will not foul the underbody of the boat. *Second*, use two anchors in line. That is, attach the kedge with a length of chain to the bower ring with a shackle. Lower the kedge first, then the bower while making sternway. Or, drop the bower first with the kedge attached at least the depth of the water distance aft on the cable, certainly no less than 7 to 8 meters distance. Remember, in any storm situation the strains on deck attachment points will be excessive. Make sure that chain cable can be released instantly if you must drop the anchor and run. Buoy the chain before releasing it.

4. Dragging can be much more than a nuisance. On a lee shore it can be deadly. If your boat begins to drag–something you can tell from reference to landmarks–start the engine first! Then pay out more cable. If this does not work, motor up, taking in cable and re-set the anchor. If the bottom is suspect, try running a riding weight down the anchor cable. This can be a patent device or a ball of chain. Just make sure that whatever weight you use is reasonably heavy, say equal to the weight of the kedge anchor. If this does not work effectively, set a second anchor at an angle of 25 to 35 degrees.

5. There are times when you will foul the anchor, either on seabed refuse or underwater cables or with another anchor. First, try hauling in cable until it is vertical and taut. Then move weight aft to try breaking it out or supply appropriate leverage via a windlass. If this doesn't work, try sailing or motoring out, pulling in the opposite direction from which the anchor was originally set. So much for the easy methods. All the rest take a certain amount of real and imaginary labor. You can run a loop of line or chain down over the anchor cable, carry it out in the dinghy and then haul from the opposite direction. Or, you can use a grapnel (or a small hook) from the *anchored* dinghy to try and pick up the main anchor, or any obstructing cable. Needless to say, a member of the crew must be stationed at the bow of the mother ship and another at its wheel to cover any possibility of backward drift. If the anchor and cable are fouled by another boat's ground tackle, attempt to raise both anchor *and* cable, securing them by a line to the boat as you lift the pair higher and higher. Then try to free the anchor by hand from the dinghy (tethered to the mother ship).

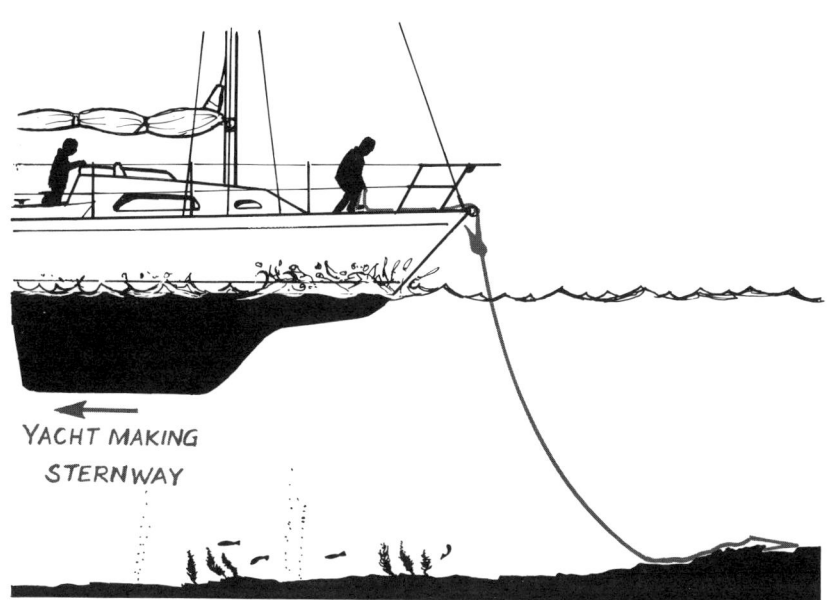

YACHT MAKING
STERNWAY

See note 3.

See note 4.

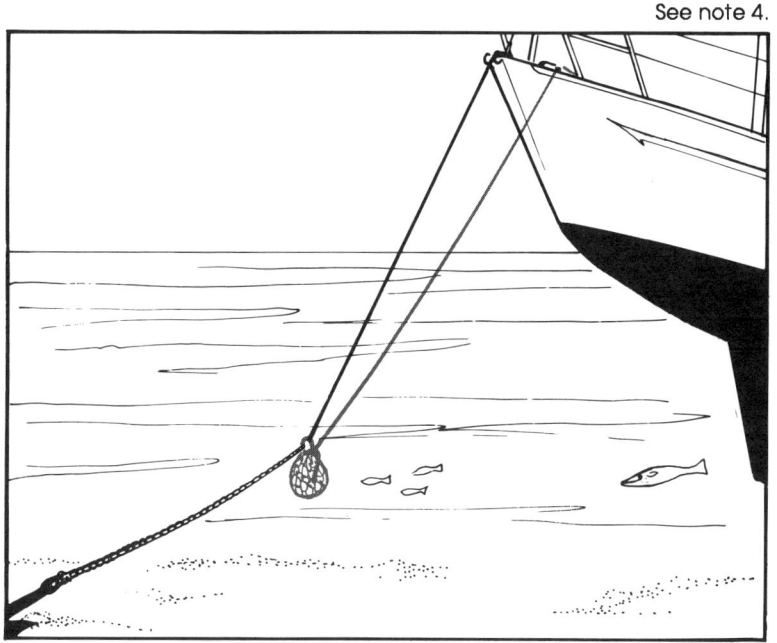

6. When the chance exists that you will be in a crowded anchorage (what isn't these days?) or expect that you shall have to depart an anchorage with greater dispatch than you had perhaps originally planned, it is a good idea to set up a buoyed trip line. Very simply, attach a length of reasonably light cordage (8mm) to the crown of the anchor before lowering it. To the "top" end, tie a short length of chain to steady it and a small buoy or plastic bottle. This will tend to keep other boats away; should the anchor become fouled, it will give you a ready-set method for breaking it free.

7. If you singlehand, setting an anchor can be a frantic experience. First, lower and secure the mainsail. You will find it much easier to handle the boat under just foresail and without the danger of swinging booms and backing sails. Pass the rode or cable outside of all stanchions and lines aft to the cockpit, making sure the cable is secured, with the necessary scope, to the foredeck. You can release both anchor and jib sheets together, calmly move forward and snub anchor and lower the jib one after the other. Release latches to drop the anchor from a roller chock are not recommended. They have a tendency to stick, or you may release the anchor and accidentally overshoot the rode, creating a large tangled mass about the underwater appendages of your boat.

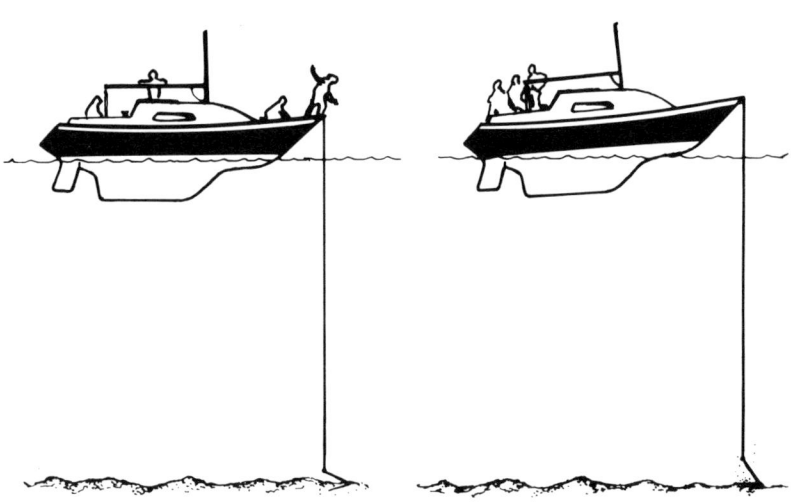

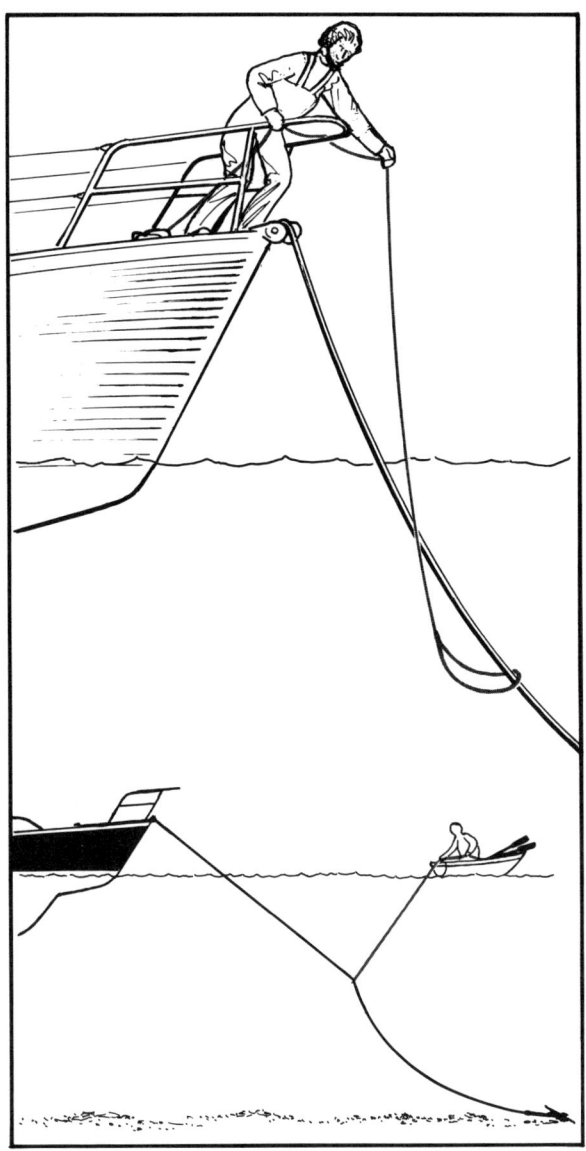

A fouled anchor can be broken free in as many ways as it can foul. One method to break it out is through intelligent manipulation of weight (left); another is to use a looped line, carried in an opposing direction by a dinghy, to reverse the pull on the rode (above).

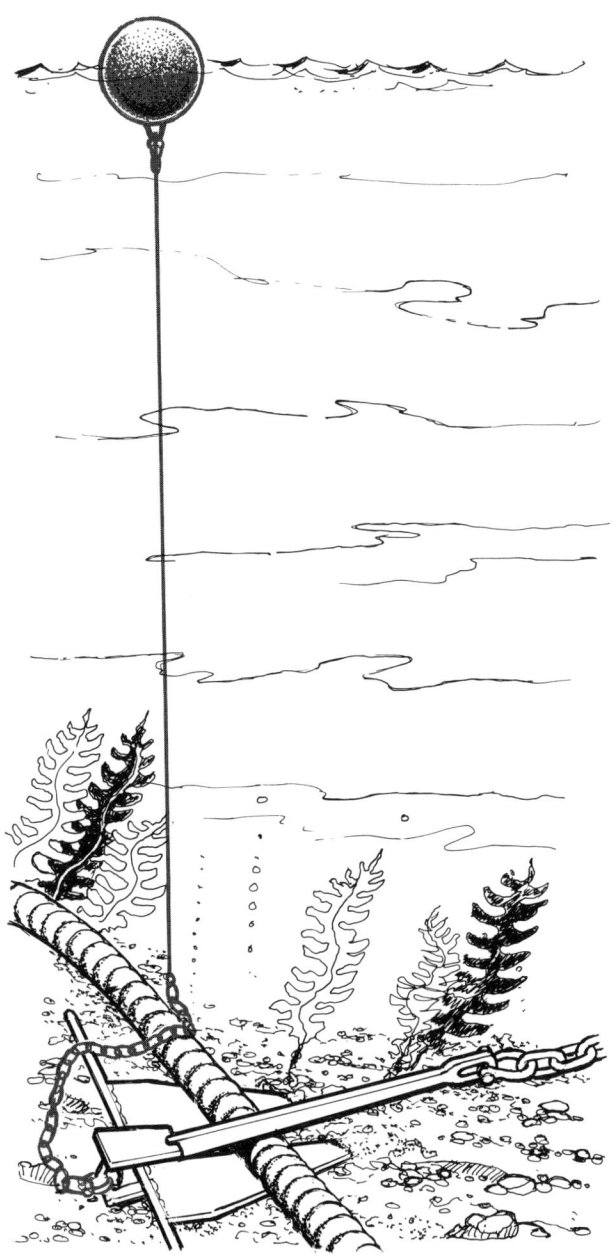

Forethought, that rarest of human commodities, will advise you to set a buoyed trip line, especially in older harbors where the seabed is sure to be littered with major mechanical debris.

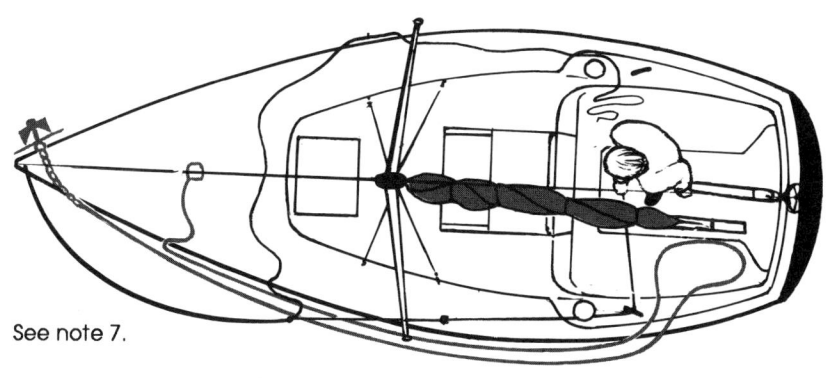

See note 7.

BOOM BREAKS

❶ USE FLAT-SIDED SPLINTS–FLOORBOARDS, FIDDLES, BUNK BOARDS–LASHED TO EITHER SIDE OF BOOM EXTENDING A COUPLE OF FEET BEYOND BREAK ON EITHER SIDE.

❷ IF THE BOOM IS SHATTERED OR FRACTURED BEYOND REPAIR, REMOVE IT AND LASH A SPINNAKER POLE, BOAT HOOK OR SUCH TO THE GOOSENECK, WITH THE MAINSAIL REEFED. TIE REEF POINTS AROUND JOCKEY BOOM.

❸ IF THE GOOSENECK RUPTURES, LASH INBOARD END OF BOOM TO MAST USING REEFING HOOKS OR ANY PROJECTION. APPLY CHAFE PROTECTION.

❹ IF ALL ELSE FAILS, AND YOU MUST SAIL WITHOUT A BOOM, REINFORCE THE CLEW AND LEAD SEPARATE SHEETS TO THE QUARTERS, THEN FORWARD TO WINCHES BY WAY OF THE SPINNAKER TURNING BLOCKS; OR, IN DESPERATION, BEND SHEETS TO CLEW FITTING, LASH AROUND THE CLEW CORNER AND LEAD AS ABOVE.

❺ SET STORM TRYSAIL.

1. If foot of mainsail leads into a groove in the boom, lashing using splints will be next to impossible. Try a boomless approach.

2. If using a substitute boom, be sure to reef the mainsail. The stress on the clew will be great and you stand a good chance of ripping the clew fitting out if you do not spread the strains along the foot by tying off reef points.

3. Lashing a boom to the mast without benefit of the gooseneck is a dangerous and never easy job. Drop the main immediately, tie down boom to prevent damage to boat and crew. Use several heavy lashings tied off independently of one another. Apply as much chafe protection as possible, especially to the inboard end of the boom.

4. Boomless jury-rigged mains are no laughing matter. You may destroy the sail without proper reinforcement. Sail shape will be distorted, and the forces on the clew will be extreme. Leads can be either to turning blocks or snatch blocks on the rail. Remember that the forces are doubled and the snatch blocks and their deck attachment points must be massively robust.

5. Storm trysails are remarkably efficient, rarely used sails. You should, of course, know how to set one, and have it in readiness and good repair with its sheets attached. Since it is designed to be used boomless, you have, in your sail locker, the perfect solution to a broken boom.

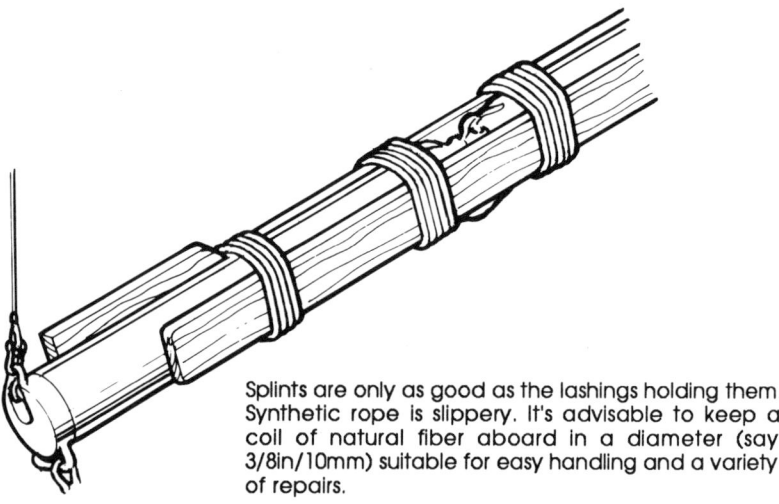

Splints are only as good as the lashings holding them. Synthetic rope is slippery. It's advisable to keep a coil of natural fiber aboard in a diameter (say 3/8in/10mm) suitable for easy handling and a variety of repairs.

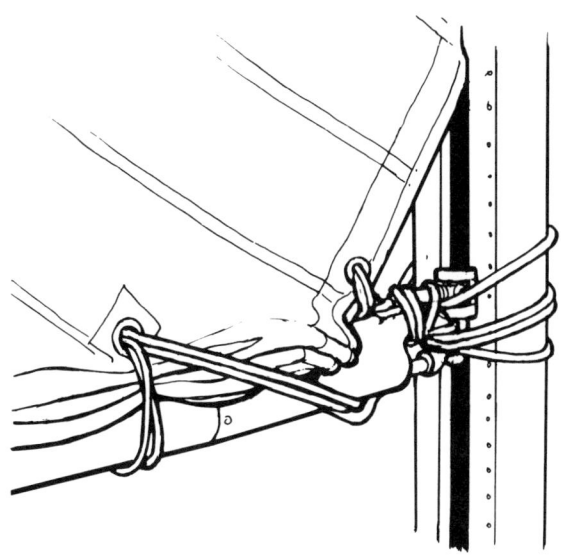

Any lashing–in the case of a broken gooseneck fitting–should be at least quadruple as chafe will be extraordinary. You must allow for twisting as well as athwartships and up-and-down movements.

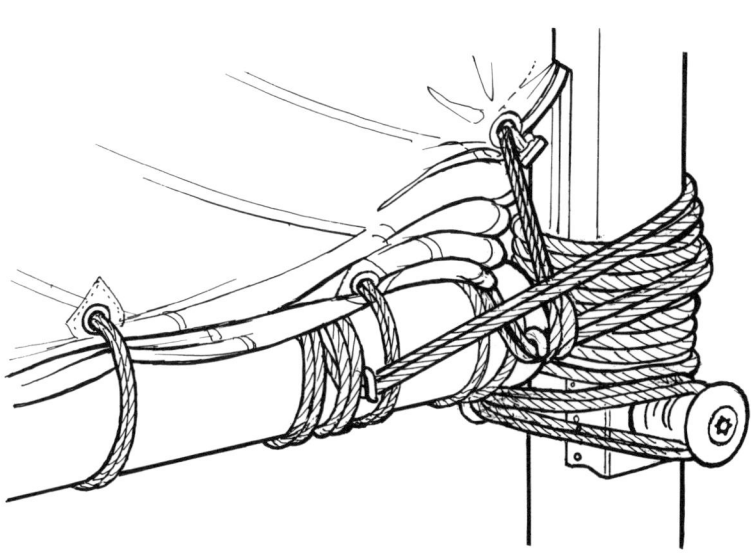

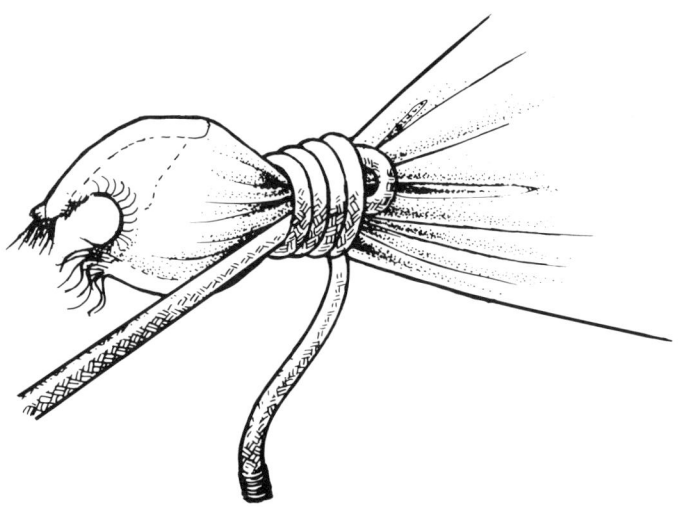

Using a lashed sail without a boom demands carefully thinking through leads. Multiple blocks may be necessary. A better solution is to rig the trysail if one is aboard.

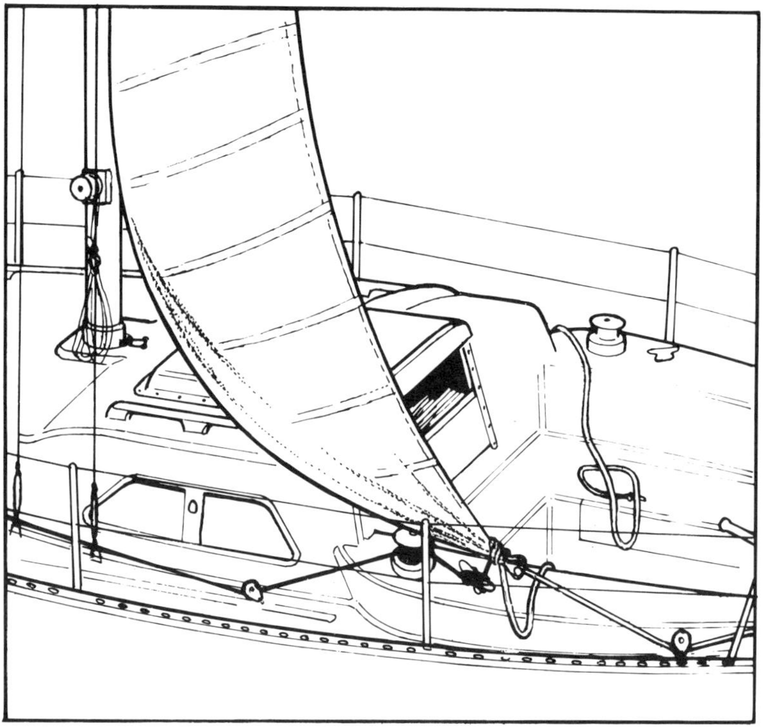

CHAFE

❶ IF BADLY CHAFED AND IN DANGER OF LETTING GO, CUT LINE AND JOIN ENDS BY A SHEETBEND OR TWO BOWLINES.

❷ IF CHAFE IS AT POINT WHERE THE LINE PASSES THROUGH A SHEAVE, REVERSE LINE END-FOR-END.

❸ TO AVOID CHAFE, PAD LINE BY VARIOUS METHODS (SEE BELOW).

❹ CUT AND SPLICE.

1. A sheetbend is the quickest way to take care of a serious chafe, though it must be remembered that knots will never be as strong as the original or as a splice. Using two bowlines will have the advantage of easy undoing of the knots no matter how heavy the strain on the lines.

2. The easiest thing to do is to end-for-end the line, although, depending on the application, this can cause further chafe and weakening of the line. However, with modern fiber rope this is rarely a problem, and top-quality polyester rope will last as long as twenty years with proper care. Better, get rid of the original cause of the chafing: unfair leads, rough edges (especially on metal fittings, the application of a fine-toothed file will achieve wonders), and so on.

3. Padding–whether plastic tubing or hose, rags, leather, a sacrificial rope whipping or baggywrinkle–is as old a practice as the sailor has. Where sail chafe is involved, the best recourse is to have the sail recut or reinforced. Baggywrinkle is ugly, soils the sails, and creates a surprising amount of windage. It is better to use shroud rollers or spreader tips. No matter what method is chosen, the padding must be secured, either with tape or whipping.

4. The most secure method of repairing a chafed line, short of replacing the line altogether, is to cut and splice it. A short splice will be stronger, but will not be able to pass through a block sheave; a long splice will be close to the original diameter of the line and will pass, providing the sheave is large enough in the first place.

Two bowlines.

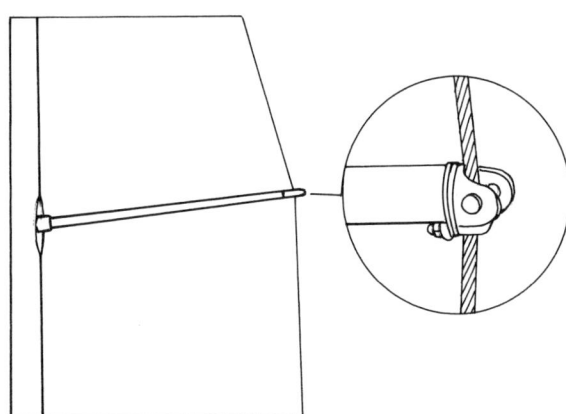

Spreaders are responsible for much sail chafe. Ends must be captive and either smoothed or taped to avoid tearing sails.

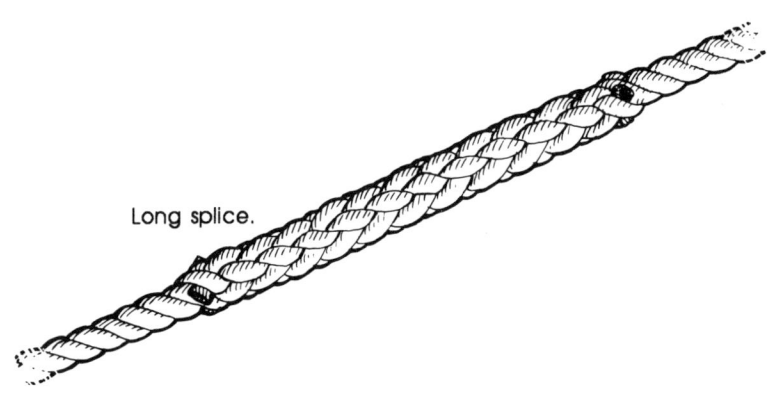

Long splice.

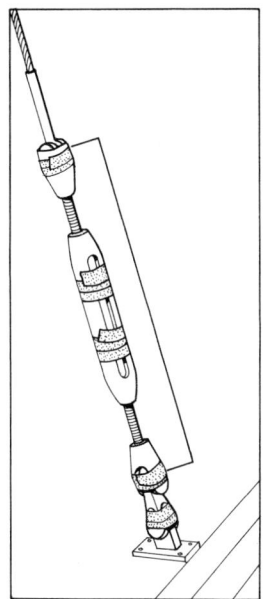 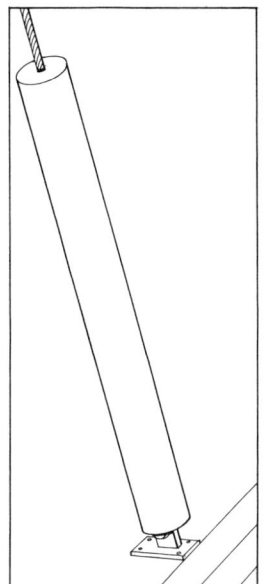 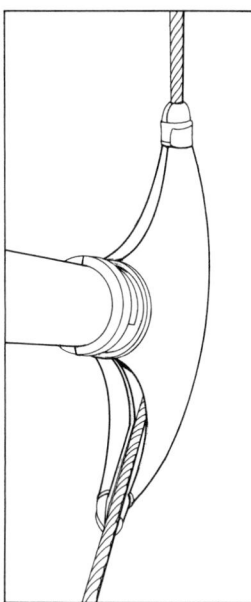

See note 3.

Top: Sheaves must be sized to the wire or rope passing over them, otherwise chafe or pinching will result.

Bottom: Rope ends should be whipped to prevent unraveling, even in synthetics.

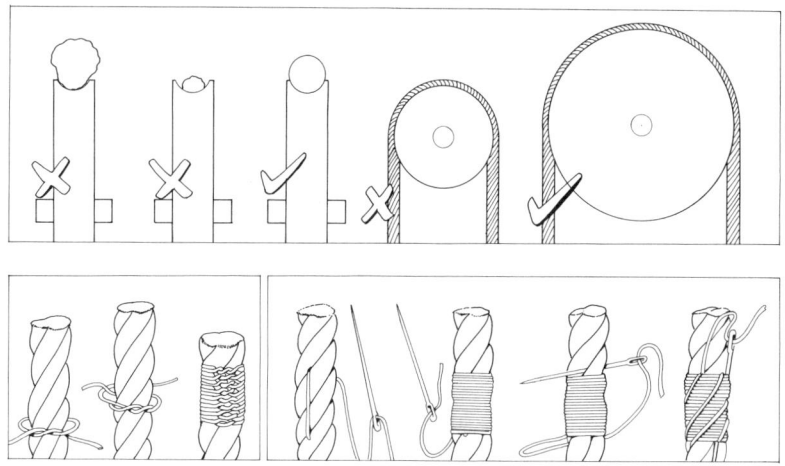

Chafe   35

COLLISION

❶ TAKE A SERIES OF BEARINGS.

❷ SIGNAL APPROPRIATELY.

❸ TAKE EVASIVE ACTION.

1. If bearings remain constant, chances are you are on a collision course. Taking bearings at night can be especially difficult. Try to keep one set of the approaching ship's range lights in line.

2. Chances are that a large ship will not spot you until after you have spotted her. You will probably have to take evasive action, but you should attempt to signal first: five or more short blasts of a horn will be taken as a warning. At night, either five short flashes of a strong light, or the Morse code "U" (2 short and 1 long flashes). Also, a torch shown against the sails or a white flare will indicate your presence.

Warning signals:
> One blast: I am altering course to starboard.
> Two blasts: I am altering course to port.
> Three blasts: I am going astern.
> Five blasts: Watch out! *or* I do not comprehend your intentions or actions.

3. Evasive action does not mean sailing until you see the whites of their eyes! Make all maneuvers with decision and positively. Course changes should be large and the new course should be held. Do *not* constantly change course; you will only confuse the oncoming ship. Always try to pass astern of the approaching vessel.

4. Despite all the rules of the road, you should not hold to etiquette. Forget everything you ever learned about sail over power, etc. You should be the one to avoid the other vessel. Especially with large ships at sea, not always, but often, the watch will be short-handed or they will not be manning the radar, in particular with flag-of-convenience registry. Right of way is only of import if the other vessel responds in kind; otherwise, assume she is going to make mincemeat of you and act accordingly. If there is a chance of a head-on collision, both vessels *should* alter their courses to starboard. If the other does not, take immediate evasive action, under the fastest means possible, full throttle ahead.

5. If a collision is unavoidable, try to present the smallest area of your ship as is possible to the oncoming vessel. This will, hopefully, lessen the impact and the resultant damage. If you are struck, the other vessel–a large tanker, say–may not even know she has hit you. Get off distress flares as fast as possible. Sound horns, bells, sirens–anything to attract attention. Have the crew stand by to abandon ship.

See note 4.

See note 5.

DINGHY

❶ DON'T OVERLOAD!

❷ STEP IN TO THE CENTER.

❸ ROW APPROPRIATELY.

❹ LAUNCH AND RETRIEVE WITH CARE.

1. More deaths are probably caused by swamped and capsized dinghies than by anything else on the water. The average tender is perhaps 8 or 10 feet in length and cannot really hold more than three people in anything but a dead calm. In truly rough water, no more than two should attempt a journey. As well as not overloading with people, you must be careful to avoid masses of gear, especially in the ends of the boat. Try to keep the boat carefully trimmed and balanced, both athwartships and fore-and-aft.

2. The novice will inevitably step on the gunwale when trying to board. This can lead to lacerations or a dunking. In most hard tenders, you can step directly into the center portion of the floorboards. However, if the dock or float is particularly high, you may have to alight on the center thwart and descend quickly. The idea is to sit down as quickly as possible, whilst the next crew member comes aboard. *Never* board a dinghy with your hands full. Either load first, or enter and have someone else hand the cargo to you once you are seated.

3. Most dinghy oars are far too short, too heavy and ill-balanced. Ideally, they should fit into the tender, be made of spruce and shaped to be comfortable to use and efficient at propelling the boat. Far too few people ever bother to learn to row properly. The beamier the boat, the shorter the strokes; the heavier the seas, the shorter the strokes is a fairly sound rule of thumb. However, load, windage, sea state, wetted surface all play a part in the best (read: most effective, least tiring) way to row. Practice. And be sure that you have oarlocks, leathers and a rowing position—with foot brace—that can stand up to the job. Trial and error will find the way.

4. Getting the dink into the water and back on board is the first concern of the cruising sailor. It must always be tethered to the mother ship. Too often a perfect launch is followed by a perfect

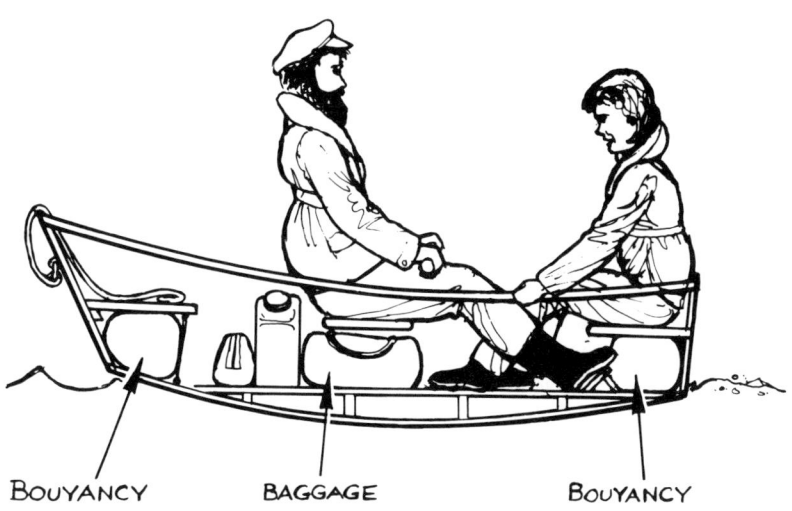

BOUYANCY   BAGGAGE   BOUYANCY

Weight distribution and balance are the keys to successful dinghy handling. More deaths are caused by failure to attend to these points than in any other area of boating.

Boarding, always step into the center of the boat, holding onto the dock or float with one hand.

drift into the distance. Obviously, the method of launching is dependent upon the ship, but usually some sort of hoist and tackle arrangement will be necessary to accomplish the job with minimum fuss and danger. Always try to have an extra hand to assist. Probably the greatest danger–other than overloading–is in landing or launching through surf. This is *never* a deed to be undertaken lightly! With oar power, the difficulty will be to restrain the dinghy enough or propel it fast enough. With an outboard, the problems are stalling, cavitation and general unreliability if swamped. And that is the danger: swamping, or capsize. If the surf is running with any power, you would be well advised to stay on the ship or beach. Otherwise, you shall need a large enough boat and crew to power through. Do not underestimate the power of breaking seas. They can crack your boat into pieces and kill you and your crew.

See note 4.

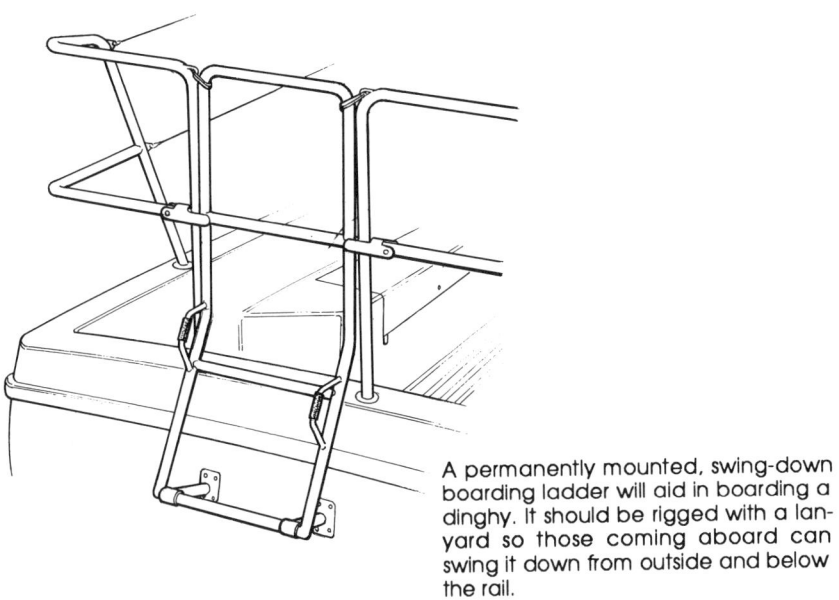

A permanently mounted, swing-down boarding ladder will aid in boarding a dinghy. It should be rigged with a lanyard so those coming aboard can swing it down from outside and below the rail.

The boom, with slings, controlled by the topping lift can be used to launch and recover the dinghy. A second person should be stationed at the rail to keep the boat clear of the topsides and to guide it aboard. The mainsheet acts as a preventer.

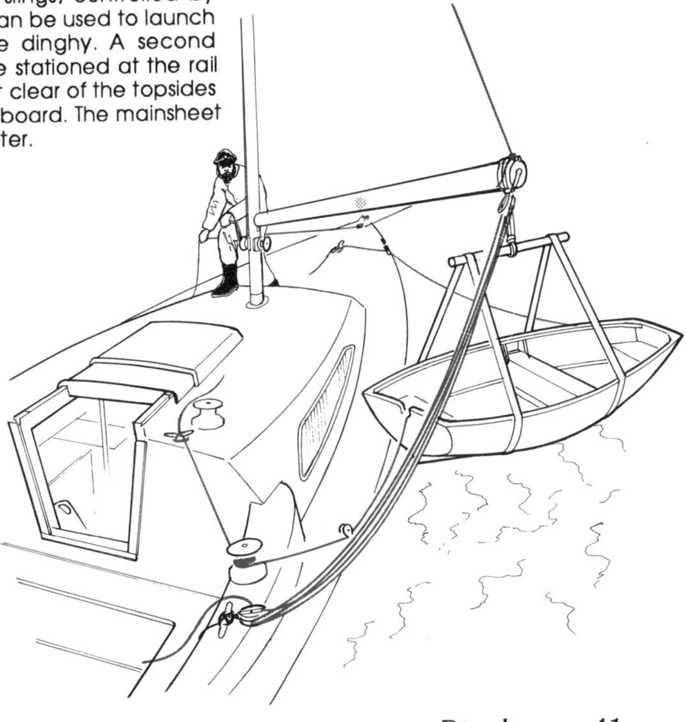

DISMASTING

❶ IF THE MAST BREAKS AT OR NEAR THE BASE, IT WILL GO OVERBOARD; IT MUST BE SECURED OR CUT LOOSE.

❷ IF THE FORESTAY PARTS WHILST BEATING, THE MAST CAN FRACTURE AND FALL AFT INTO THE COCKPIT.

❸ IF THE MAST BREAKS AT THE SPREADERS, IT MUST BE UN-TANGLED AND A JURY RIG SET.

❹ NO MATTER WHAT, IMMEDIATE ACTION WILL BE NECES-SARY!

1. A mast that has gone overboard presents a serious threat to the continuing integrity of the hull, especially in heavy weather. In calm seas, you and the crew may be able to hoist the mast back on board. If the mast is sizeable and therefore heavy, a better procedure will be to lash it to the hull. Hoisting will necessitate securing the spar on at least three points along its length, and rigging tackles fore, aft and amidships, using winches in the cockpit, perhaps the vang to the maststep and the anchor windlass with appropriate jury-rigged fairleads. Station crew at each location and be sure that the hull is appropriately fendered; in this instance, *every* fender aboard should be secured to the rail on the hoisting side. Chances are that the lifelines and stanchions went by the board when the mast went over, so safety harnesses are *de rigueur*. Since most masts will add considerable weight to the side to which they have been lashed, it may be necessary, especially in a light-displacement boat, to rearrange the stores and weights below deck. In addition, metal masts, unless foam-filled, will sink fairly quickly. It is imperative to move with dispatch.

2. If you decide to lash the mast to the side of the yacht, a large part of the rigging will have to be cut away. This can be done either by undoing the rigging screws (which will most likely be bent out of shape by the shock) or by cutting the rigging wires, either with cable cutters or with a cold chisel and hammer against a steel block. Be warned: rod rigging will not be so easy to part. That rigging which can be left—lower shrouds on the side of the vessel on which the mast went over—should be kept as added security. Remember, however, that it may be necessary, in increasingly heavy weather, to cut the mast adrift. Those remaining attachment points will hamper any efforts to do so.

A mast gone overboard must be either cut away completely or secured to the vessel. Both procedures are extremely hazardous. See note 1.

3. An additional thought: the mast can be left trailing from bow or stern to act as a sea anchor. In truly atrocious seas, this may well be the best way to retain some steerage and control. This must be accompanied by constant watch, for the errant spar could well be flung onto the ship by breaking seas. In such a case, the mast should be secured with rope cordage, rather than by rigging wire, since cutting it loose if necessary will be much simplified if an axe can take precedence over a pair of cutters.

4. Should the mast fall aft, chances are the crew in the cockpit will be injured, wheel or tiller will be broken, the cabin house may fracture. Get any injured crew below and commence appropriate first aid. The mast should probably be cut away as soon as possible. If the steering mechanism is broken see JURY RIGS: RUDDER, TILLER: BREAKAGE, etc.

5. Breaks at the spreaders are more common than one would wish to imagine. Due to the number of fittings, terminals, etc., at that point, the mast can be weakened. If the mast should fracture and the upper portion come tumbling down, lash it to deck and proceed to JURY RIGS: MASTS. If the mast is left dangling, lash the upper part to the portion left standing; trying to cut down the top and maneuver it to the deck can be a tricky and dangerous job.

6. Move fast to avoid damage to the ship, but not so fast as to endanger the crew. Think out your actions first and instruct the crew carefully and clearly on what must be done.

See note 2.

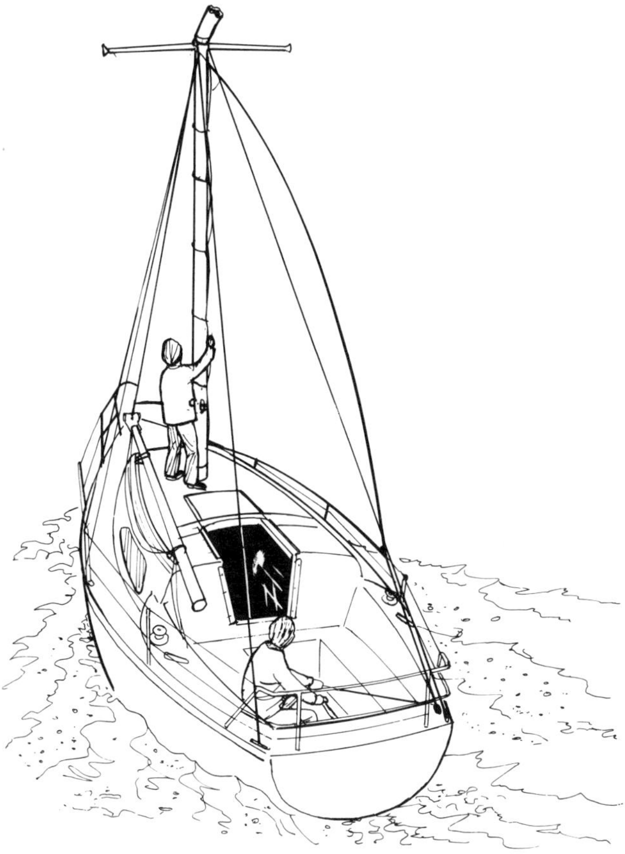

A mast broken at the spreaders can be used as the basis of a jury rig. See JURY RIGS: MAST.

See note 3.

DIVING

❶ ANCHOR OR HEAVE TO.

❷ SECURE THE PERSON DIVING WITH A LINE.

❸ ARRANGE SIGNALS.

❹ ALWAYS HAVE SOMEONE STANDING BY ON DECK.

1. Attempting to dive when the boat is in motion is foolhardy in the extreme. Any additional movement will make any underwater task extraordinarily difficult for the diver. The most usual reason for having to dive is either to unfoul the anchor or to clear the propeller. In either case *be sure the ignition is off*!

2. Since few people can remain underwater without artificial breathing apparatus for more than 45 seconds to one minute, especially when exerting themselves, a safety line is a must.

3.The person on deck should have prearranged signals with the diver: one jerk on the line, pull up; two jerks, help; etc.

4. A line without a tender is useless. The person on deck will often sight danger before the diver: shark approaching, squall coming, etc.

5. Always have a boarding ladder secured before the diver goes in. He will know where it is and there will be no fumbling when it is needed. Make it as long as possible and weight the bottom rung.

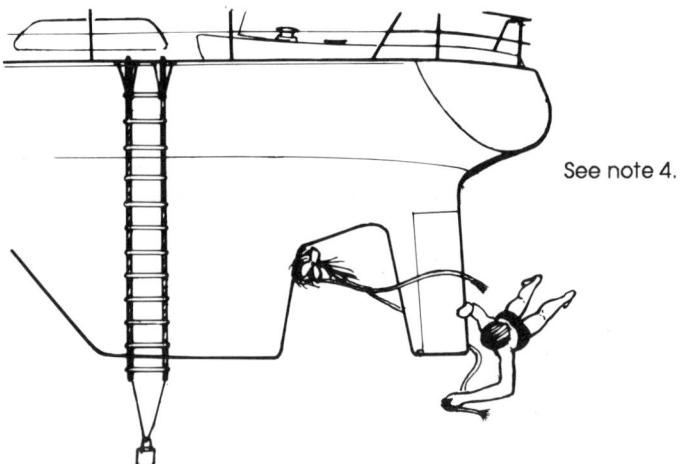

See note 4.

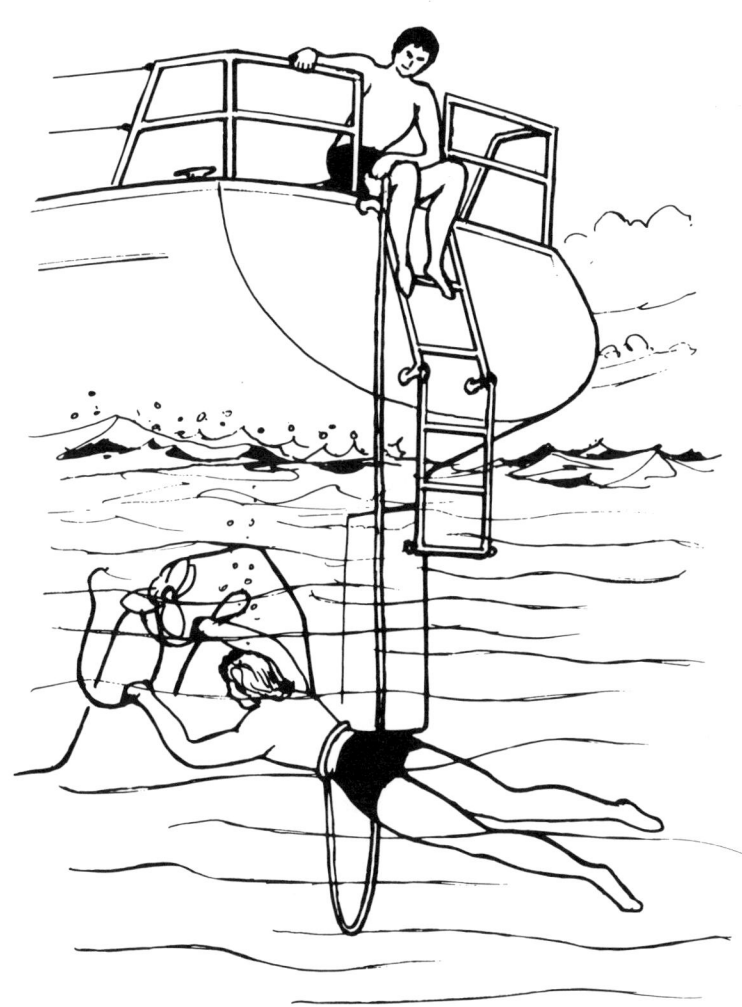

Safety lines are a must when working underwater without scuba gear. Even then, a line for signaling is recommended. Always wear goggles when working below to protect one's eyes.

DOCKING

❶ APPROACH WITH CAUTION.

❷ HAVE ALL LINES AND FENDERS PREPARED AND CORRECTLY POSITIONED.

❸ BE PREPARED TO CHANGE SIDE OF APPROACH QUICKLY.

1. Approaching any dock or quay or pontoon is made more difficult by the tight quarters, proximity of other vessels and the tricks tidal streams can play amongst pilings and walls. Make due allowance for windage, drift and lost control at low speeds. Know how your ship handles! Attempt to approach to windward. With wind and tide behind you, you will have to either play with bursts of reverse on the throttle or have a crew member stationed to drop a stern anchor to slow down the ship and allow for some control. The same maneuver can be practiced with current abeam.

2. Cleat all lines and pass through chocks, then outboard and over any rails or lifelines. Secure all fenders overboard. If approaching a concrete or stone pier, use fenderboards. Often the pier will be quite high; a crew member should be stationed so he can scale the wall (hopefully by ladder) with both bow *and* stern lines in hand. The same is true if sailing alone or with one crew. Spring lines can be rigged after bow and stern are secured. Should the ship be tied up on the windward side of the dock, a kedge can be run out to hold it off, either from a spring cleat amidships or with two warps leading from the kedge to both bow and stern cleats.

3. You could suddenly have to alter your intended approach or goal, either due to the unexpected appearance of a smaller, hitherto unseen boat, or to directions from the dockmaster. Lines, fenders, etc., will have to be quickly switched. If you have enough time, it pays to back off and reapproach *after* these chores have been completed. If not, and the area is crewed on first approach, it is a good idea to rig lines and fenders on both sides of the yacht. In places like St. Peter Port or Newport or Annapolis, at the height of the season, docking is always at a premium. Plan accordingly.

4. In most of the Mediterranean, tying up stern-to is the norm. This is accomplished by letting out the best bower about 100 feet (30m) plus the length of the ship from the quay and backing toward the dock. Unfortunately, with adverse conditions this can be at

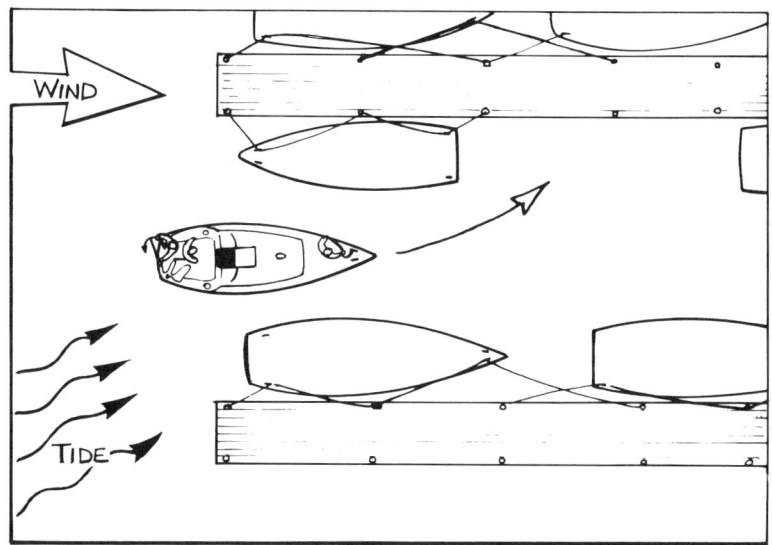

See note 1.

See note 2.

HEAVE II

Docking   49

best a tricky maneuver. Better to drop the hook from the stern and go in bow first. Most boats have greater control in forward, as well as greater stopping power. In addition, should you desire such things, your privacy will be that much more. If you wish you can end-for-end the bow and anchor lines–providing there is room port and starboard–and turn the ship around. If boats are wedged in on both sides, extend the line to the quay and haul well clear of your neighbors before attempting to make the turn.

5. Should the berth be one that dries out at low tide, attempt to heel the boat slightly inward toward the quay. A line passed about the mast at spreader height and led ashore will usually do the trick. Be careful that the rigging does not come in contact with the dock, and that the spreaders will not be damaged. A block attached to a halyard and also held around the mast with a strop or loose loop of rope can be hoisted aloft to just below the spreaders *after* a line from the dock has been led through it and back to the dock or to a cleat on deck. In addition, a heavy anchor can be placed on the dockside deck of the vessel.

6. Be sure in any tidal area that enough slack is kept in the docking line to allow for the rise and fall of the ship. A good idea is to lead the lines to the dock pilings or cleats in a bight and then back again to the deck cleats. In this manner, you will be able to make adjustments without leaving the deck.

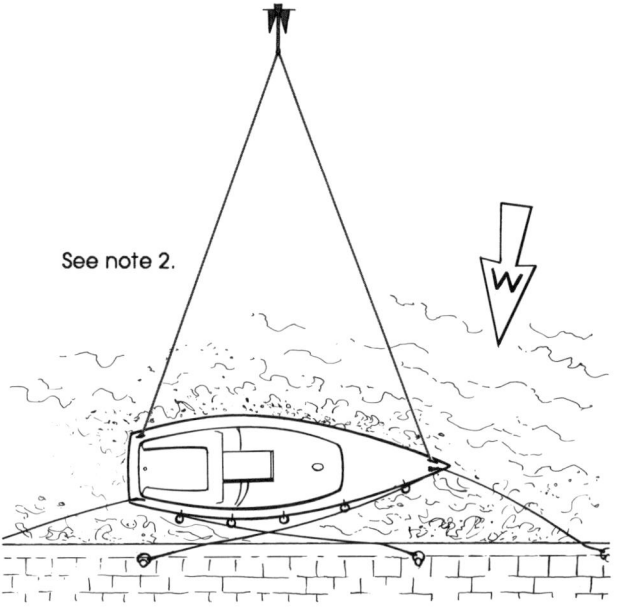

See note 2.

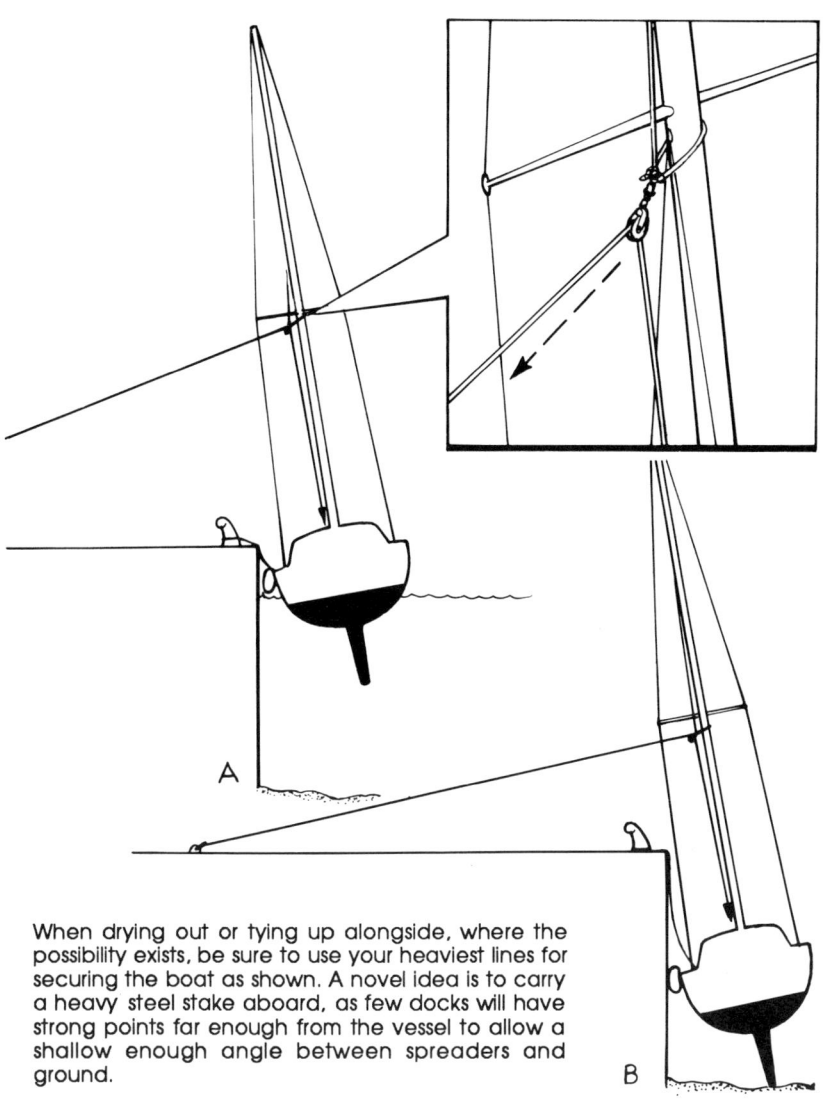

When drying out or tying up alongside, where the possibility exists, be sure to use your heaviest lines for securing the boat as shown. A novel idea is to carry a heavy steel stake aboard, as few docks will have strong points far enough from the vessel to allow a shallow enough angle between spreaders and ground.

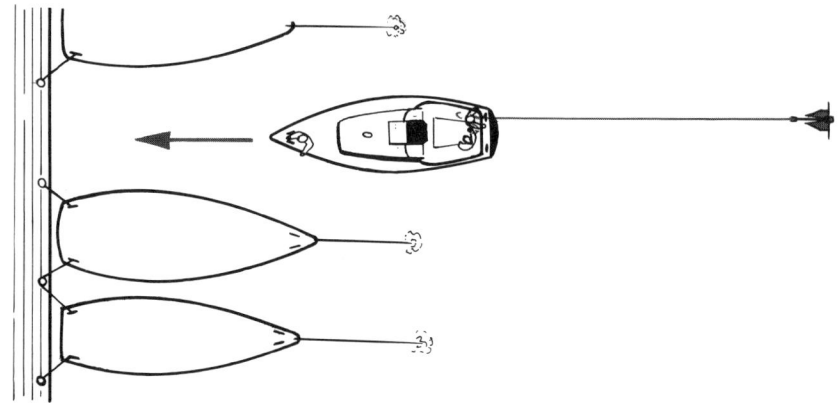

See note 4.

See note 6. Additionally, this method of tying up will
allow you to skip moorings without anyone having to
leap aboard at the last minute.

ELECTRICS

❶ LIGHTS FAIL.

❷ ENGINE WON'T START.

❸ NO POWER AT ALL!

1. It is a sorry fact of life afloat that sooner or later salt air and moisture will have a detrimental effect on your boat's electrical system. You can guard against run-of-the-mill failure by checking all connections, wiring, fuses, junction boxes, circut breakers, battery installations, etc., at the commencement of every season and at least twice during the course of the season. Battery terminals must be cleaned and, after reconnecting, coated with a thin layer of waterproof grease. Check all wire clips to see that no breaks have occurred in the insulation. Any wires running low in the ship, especially in the bilges, should be rerouted away from any possible water contamination. Overhaul the alternator and generator. Replace all fuses and lamp bulbs once a year as a matter of course. See that all connections and connecting clips are free from corrosion and coated after cleaning and reassembly. Top up batteries and secure. Make sure they are properly vented. Check engine wiring harnesses and make sure all wires are securly clipped and away from any excessive heat sources.

2. Assuming you have done all the above and the power fails, what do you do? First check the battery. It may be dry. A connection may be vibrated or torn loose. The alternator may not be functioning. A fuse may be blown, or a cable may have shorted out.

3. Having checked the above, and found the situation beyond repair, the following are all reasonable alternatives: Use a kerosene/paraffin lantern hung in the rigging instead of navigation lights. At worst you will be thought a fisherman! Or use an electric/battery anchor light. If the engine has no handcrank starting capability, and a second battery is available, jump or reconnect the cables. Sail.

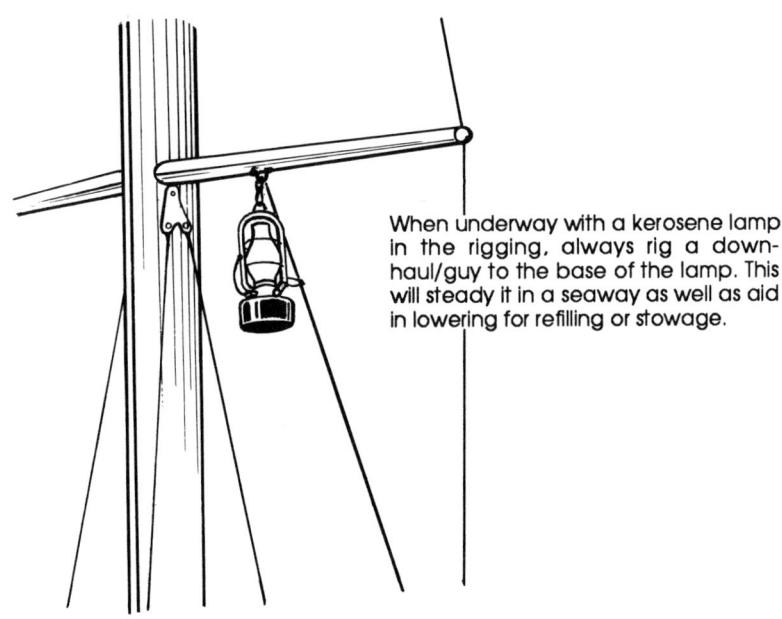

When underway with a kerosene lamp in the rigging, always rig a down-haul/guy to the base of the lamp. This will steady it in a seaway as well as aid in lowering for refilling or stowage.

Most vessels will be fitted with two batteries. A spare battery should be chocked in place. Remember that a generator and converter can be used to charge a dead battery.

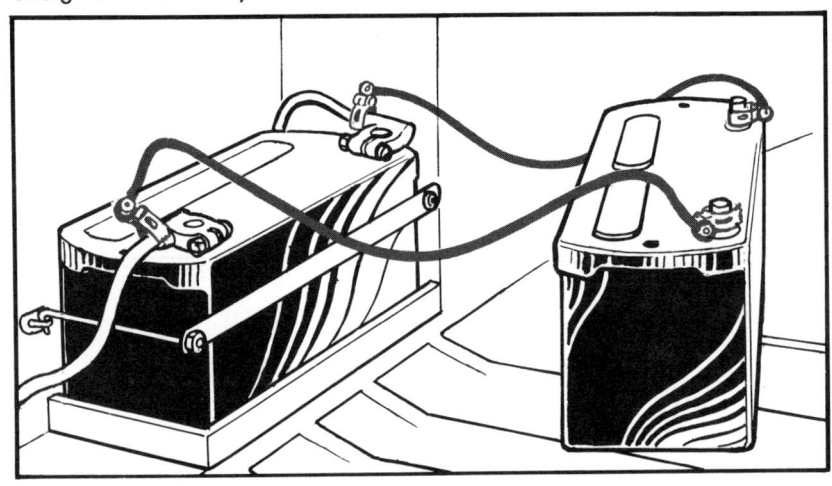

ENGINE FAILURE: *Diesel*

❶ ENGINE STOPS.

❷ ENGINE IS OVERHEATING.

❸ OIL PRESSURE DROPS.

❹ ENGINE RUNS UNEVENLY.

❺ IN ALL THE ABOVE CASES, STOP ENGINE!

1. If the engine stops on its own accord, switch off the ignition. Check the fuel system. Filters must be free of dirt and water. They should be filled with oil. The possibility exists that the tanks are empty. The filters may be only partly filled if this is the case. However, partial filter filling may also be due to a fuel line blockage. If the engine won't restart, you will have to bleed both filters and possibly injectors. Consult your owner's manual.

2. Overheating is the most common problem with diesels and is most often the result of a torn or failed water-cooling pump impeller. First, though, check the water inlet for debris and blockage to the water pump and make sure the propeller is not fouled. This is the place to warn you: *always carry a spare impeller.* Changing it is a ten-minute job at most, but for want of a spare, you may be disabled until you can signal for a tow (in a powerboat) or the breeze picks up.

Additionally, overheating may be due to a blockage in the raw water inlet or within the cooling system itself. Check the inlet, make sure exhaust water is being discharged through the exhaust pipe. Check all water piping going to and coming from the engine for leaks. You may be able to repair minor leaks with heat welding tape or even duct tape. Major leaks or cracks will demand replacement of the piping. It's a good idea to carry lengths of heat resistant, reinforced neoprene hose in the proper diameters for just such cases. Also make adjustable stainless steel hose clips.

3. Oil pressure dropping can indicate a major problem. Check the oil level and top up. If water has mixed with the oil, the head gasket may have ruptured. Do not run the engine above very low rpms (no higher than 1500 rpm in most modern marine diesels). If there should be a crack in the crankcase, shut down the engine at once. Without proper lubrication the engine stands a good chance of seizing or grinding itself to bits.

4. If the engine will not start, yet the starter motor is turning over, the glow plug may need replacement.

5. Uneven running may be due to a clogged or broken injector. If possible, replace; if not, run engine very slowly.

6. A full spare kit as well as the manufacturer's manual should be aboard for anything more than a day sail. Read the manual before setting out on a cruise. Make sure you have the necessary tools on board. As mentioned above, should anything seem wrong–high temperature, rough running, frequent stoppages, oil pressure fluctuations–*stop the engine immediately*! Failure to do so may cause major damage. Remember that anything that moves needs maintenance. As much as you might hate the "iron jib," it is part of the yacht and needs the same care as the brightwork and winches.

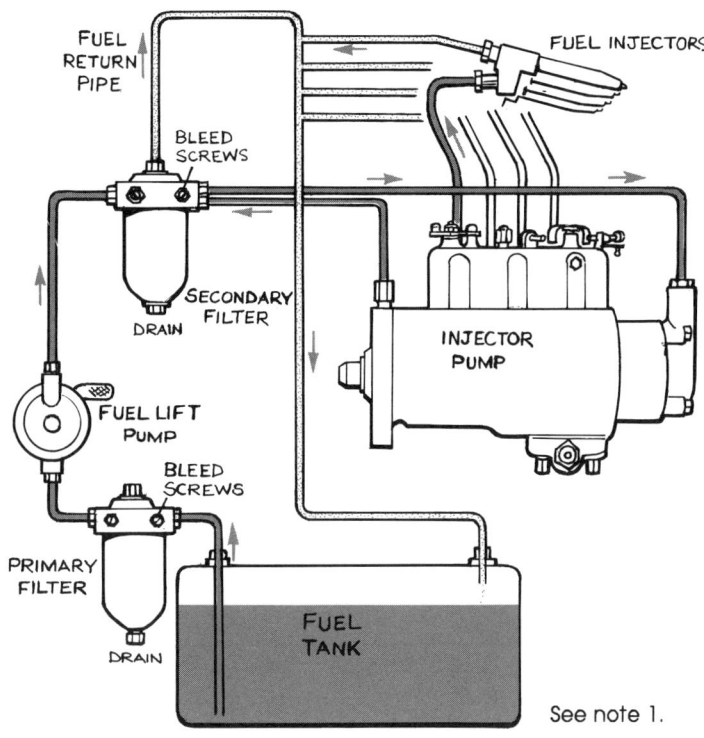

See note 1.

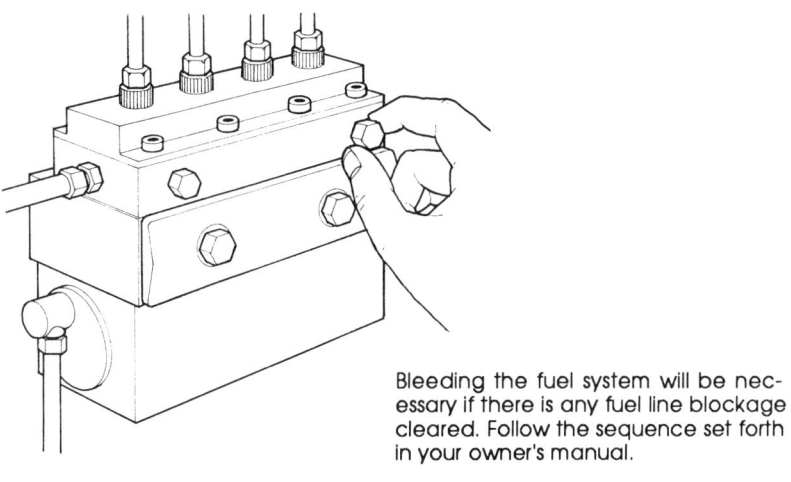

Bleeding the fuel system will be necessary if there is any fuel line blockage cleared. Follow the sequence set forth in your owner's manual.

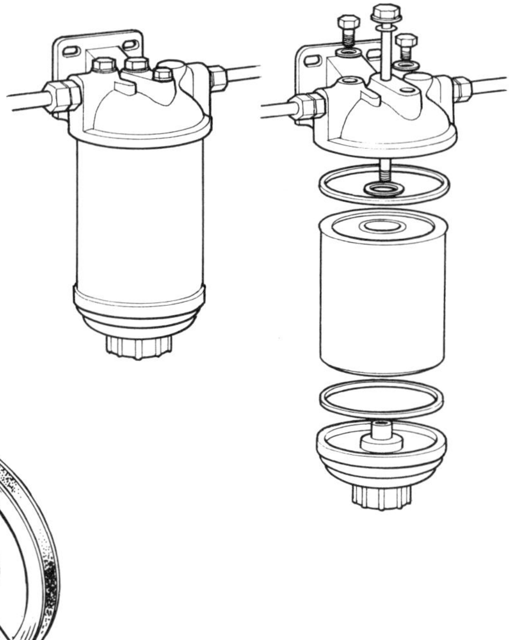

Diesel fuel systems should be fitted with at least two in-line fuel filters. Elements should be changed regularly as any foreign matter in the combustion process can clog or damage injectors.

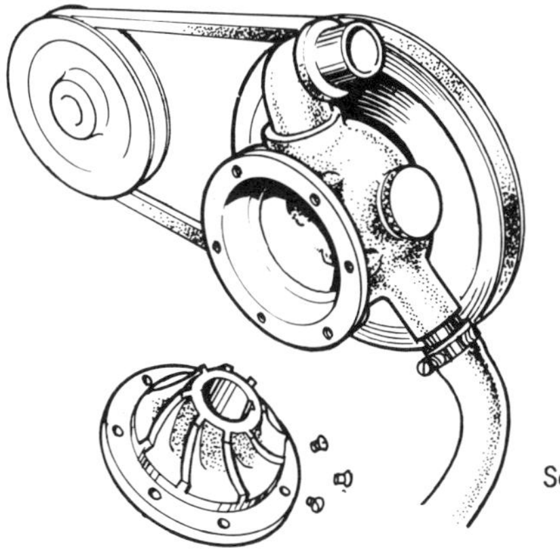

See note 2.

ENGINE FAILURE: Gas

❶ ENGINE WILL NOT START.

❷ ENGINE STOPS.

❸ ENGINE IS OVERHEATING.

❹ OIL PRESSURE DROPS.

❺ ENGINE RUNS UNEVENLY.

1. Check the electrical system. The battery may be dead, especially if the starter motor will not turn over. A connection between the battery ignition switch and starter motor circuit may be defective. Check the spark plugs and distributor head. Often, only the plugs will have to be cleaned or replaced; always carry spares.

2. If the engine stops with grinding and clanking noises, serious damage is probably at hand. If no noise occurs, an electrical fault is probable and should be traced as above. If the engine hesitates and stops, the fault is most likely with the fuel system. Check as per instruction manual. The fuel tank may be empty. If not, there is probably a blockage in the line, or the fuel pump may have malfunctioned. Blow out the fuel line. If still no result, dismantle or replace the pump. Additionally, the carburetor may need adjustment. If you have the tools and expertise, go ahead.

3. Overheating will be caused by a blocked water inlet, a broken pump, low oil level or a fouled propeller. In any case, if the temperature rises, turn off the engine immediately.

4. If there's a drop in oil pressure, stop the engine and check the oil level. Refill as necessary. Do not run the engine unless absolutely necessary.

5. Uneven running is probably due to a fouled plug or bad timing. Replace the plug. If unevenness persists, have the mechanic check it out. An obvious cause is a loose HT lead. Make sure all leads are firmly seated on the plug ends.

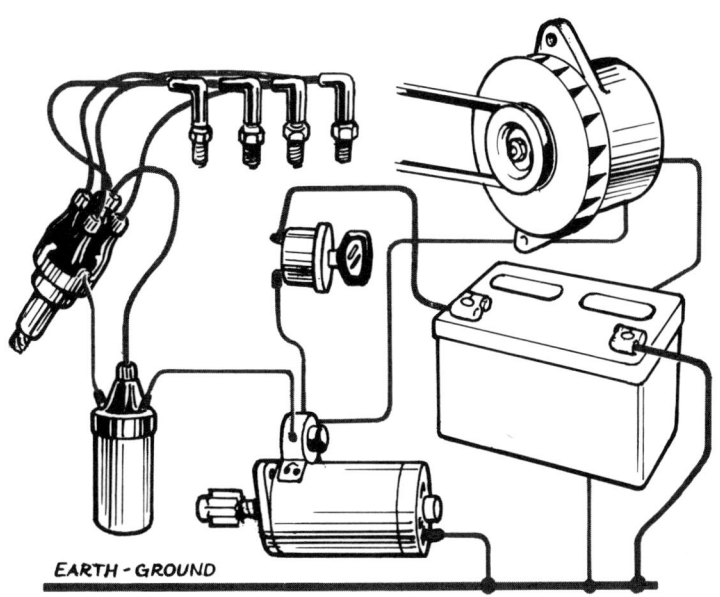

EARTH - GROUND

See note 1.

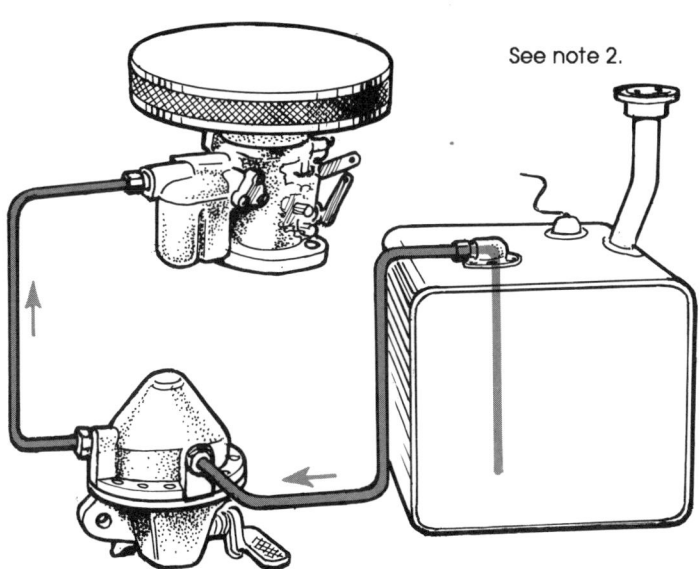

See note 2.

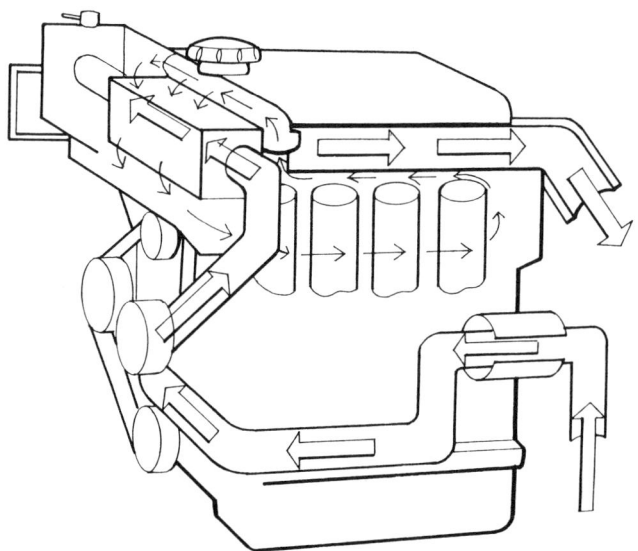

Engine cooling systems must be kept free-flowing for optimum performance. Flushing on a regular basis will help. Always check exhausts for free-flowing water. This is a generally reliable check that the cooling system is functioning.

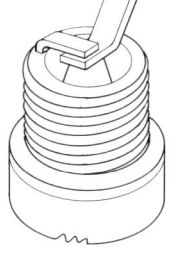 

When installing new spark plugs, gap them to manufacturer's instructions. Do not assume they have been pregapped. Failure to do so will lead to hot running and fouling.

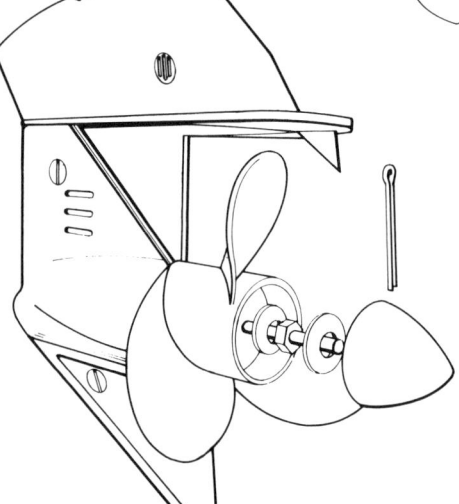

Should the outboard lower unit strike an underwater object, chances are the shear pin will have to be replaced. When making the change, pack well with waterproof grease and also replace the cotter pin.

FIRE: Engine

❶ SHUT OFF IGNITION IMMEDIATELY! CLOSE FUEL VALVE IMMEDIATELY!

❷ IF ENGINE ROOM IS EQUIPPED WITH SELF-ACTIVATING EXTINGUISHING SYSTEM, STAND BY WITH AN APPROPRIATE HAND-OPERATED UNIT. VALVES HAVE BEEN KNOWN TO CORRODE AT SEA.

❸ IF ENGINE ROOM IS EQUIPPED WITH HALON EXTINGUISHING UNIT, CLOSE EXHAUST VALVE AS SOON AS POSSIBLE (EVEN BEFORE SHUTTING OFF IGNITION), AS HALON CAN BE SUCKED OUT THROUGH THE ENGINE BEFORE IT CAN WORK EFFECTIVELY.

❹ IF NO AUTOMATIC UNIT IS INSTALLED, SHUT OFF IGNITION AND FUEL VALVE, OPEN COMPANIONWAY STEPS OR ENGINE HOUSING, STANDING WELL CLEAR IN CASE OF BURST OF FLAME. AIM EXTINGUISHER TOWARD FIRE AND RELEASE, HOLDING IT AS STEADY AS POSSIBLE.

1. It is vital to stop both fuel supply and ignition as soon as possible. This is especially true of gasoline/petrol engines, as explosion can occur both within the engine and back to the fuel tanks which, since they are usually located beneath or alongside the cockpit, can cause serious injury or death.

2. Please, please inspect and, if necessary, replace all engine room extinguisher valves at least twice each season. Since engine spaces are usually the most ignored places aboard–at least on sailing vessels–they are subject to all the ills of bad boat husbandry: oil accumulation, severe damp, grit and old rags. Valves can not only be corroded, they can be blocked by grease and debris. Likewise, all wiring for all systems should be kept clear of the bilges, not run near or over working or hot parts of the engine, secured carefully and have all terminal fittings lightly coated with waterproof grease. If any of these precautions are ignored, very likely the system will fail when you most need it.

3. Using hand-operated extinguishers is not difficult, but does demand calm and intelligence. Everyone on board should be thoroughly acquainted with their operation, and you should have fired one off in practice, with crew present. The important thing is to

hold them steady, pointed directly at the source of the flame. If necessary, brace yourself against a bulkhead or counter.

4. Engines are, of course, rarely out in the open. They are covered by hatches, companion steps or casings. If you are in the cockpit when the fire commences, get below before you open the engine compartment. You will not be able to direct your firefighting from above and unless there is a readily removable engine hatch in the cockpit sole, don't try! Actually, cockpit engine hatches probably should not be opened, as the flames shooting out will be sure to burn someone.

5. If the fire gets out of control while you are below, *Do not attempt to escape through the companionway!* Use the forward hatch, and prepare to abandon ship. In the event of *any* fire, have the crew prepare the life raft or dinghy to stand by. Unless you are aboard a steel or aluminum boat, the chances of a runaway blaze not causing the boat to founder are minimal. Fiberglass, unless laminated with fire-retardant resins, will soon turn into an inferno. If you cannot retain the fire, don't fight in vain. *Get off the boat!*

See note 3.

See note 5.

FIRE: Stove

❶ SHUT OFF FUEL VALVES IMMEDIATELY!

❷ ALCOHOL AND KEROSENE (METHS AND PARAFFIN) FIRES: SMOTHER WITH FIREPROOF BLANKET.

❸ ALCOHOL (METHS) CAN BE PUT OUT WITH WATER. HOWEVER, WATER CAN ALSO SPREAD THE FIRE.

❹ SOLID FUEL FIRES: USE WATER OR SAND.

❺ DIESEL: USE DRY POWDER OR CHEMICAL FIRE EXTINGUISHER.

❻ PROPANE, BUTANE, CNG: USE EXTINGUISHER.

1. Both stove and tank valves must be closed. If stove valve cannot be reached because of flames, shut off tank valve and attempt to rip out hose. Some modern installations have remote control valves, either mechanical or electrical. These can be wired to simultaneously cut the fuel supply at both of the valve locations.

2. Alcohol, though rarely used except in the USA, has a low flash point and can be extinguished with water. However, the splashing water can also carry flaming alcohol with it, possibly igniting curtains, upholstery or even the container of spirits used for preheating the burners.

3. Fiberglass or other flame-retardant treated blankets can often successfully be used to smother flames. They must be close at hand.

4. Wood and coal fires can, of course, be put out with water. However, it may be handier to keep a container of sand nearby. It will be safer–no steam–and usually easier to clean up afterward. This applies to both heating and cooking stoves.

5. Propane and other gas fires are the most dangerous. Flames can travel these fuel lines much faster than with other fuels. A failsafe device must be fitted to the stove, and every precaution must be made to keep all equipment in prime operating condition. Explosion is the greatest risk. If a flare-up occurs, immediately shut off the gas and apply a fire extinguisher. Use the utmost caution when lighting a gas stove. Constantly check the system for gas leaks. With the exception of compressed natural gas (CNG) the entire class of fuels is heavier than air, and can be ignited by the simple act of striking a wrench against the engine block.

6. Keep the stove clean! A grease fire can cause just as much damage as any other. Either smother or use a fire extinguisher.

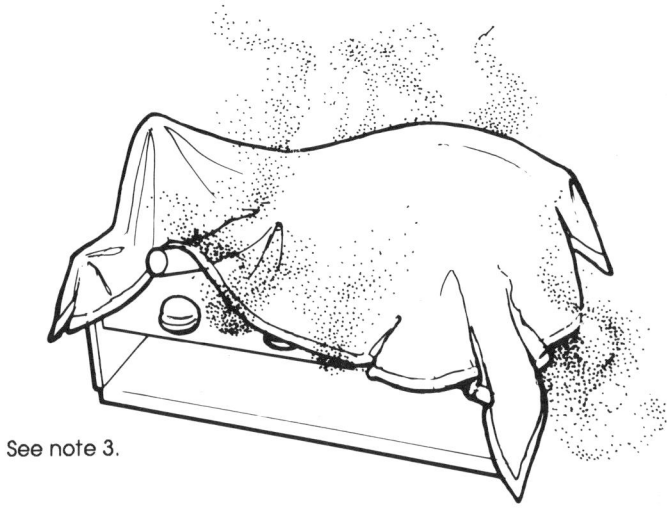

See note 3.

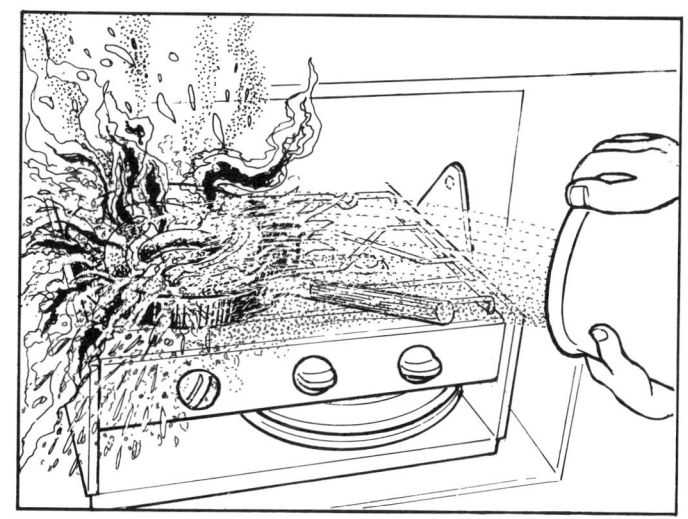

See note 2.

See note 5.

See note 4.

FOG

❶ REDUCE SPEED IMMEDIATELY!

❷ IF ON A COMPASS COURSE, ADHERE TO THAT COURSE.

❸ SOUND APPROPRIATE SIGNALS.

❹ IF POSITION IS KNOWN, CONSIDER USING DEPTH SOUNDER FOR CONTOUR NAVIGATION.

❺ IF RADAR IS ABOARD, FOLLOW THE APPROPRIATE MEASURES.

❻ POST A LOOKOUT FORWARD.

1. Fog is usually accompanied by little or no wind. However, there are times and places where dense fog will coexist with strong breezes. In such situations, decrease throttle if under power or reduce sail more than you would normally. In dense fogs, visibility may be down to less than 100 meters, and anything other than dead slow ahead poses a real threat to the vessel and crew.

2. Human senses become less than reliable in foggy conditions: sounds are distorted, shapes appear and disappear, ships creep in and out of banks that suddenly close in. The only reliable navigational tool in such situations is the traditional ship's compass. Of course, you have made sure it is corrected and compensated before setting out. TRUST IT! No matter what your senses indicate, the compass is a safer bet. It is not subject to psychological pressures, it doesn't drink, and it won't fall overboard.

3. Fog signals: international rules:
      One blast: I am turning to starboard.
      Two blasts: I am turning to port.
      Three blasts: I am going astern.
      Five blasts: Beware! I am in doubt about your intentions.
      Short, long, short blasts: Warning! Danger of collision.
These are to be sounded on a horn or whistle. The ringing of a bell signifies a vessel aground or at anchor.

Never trust your senses in a fog. A crewmember should always be posted forward as lookout while the boat moves dead slow ahead. All signaling from the bows should be by hand and in silence as hearing is a vital sense in fog.

4. If attempting to home in on an audible signal, remember that fog can distort apparent sound direction. Proceed with utmost caution.

5. Always post the best-sighted person in the bows. He will be able to give some warning of impending danger. Prearrange signals with the helmsman.

6. Contour navigation–following a sounding line on the chart–can be most useful in fog conditions. You *must* know your position, and must have an accurate, calibrated depth finder aboard, as well as an adjusted compass with deviation table. You then proceed to take soundings in a continuous run in the charted direction. Any deviation from the charted sounding line will become immediately apparent from the soundings. One person should man the chart and depth sounder and call out bearings, course and soundings to the helmsman.

7. Radar is not often found aboard small yachts, but recent developments are putting it in the range of affordability; and scanner size and power requirements are decreasing. Radar takes practice, but if you have a set, you will no doubt have figured out how to use it. Depending on range, it can show you exactly what is ahead of you in most, if not all conditions.

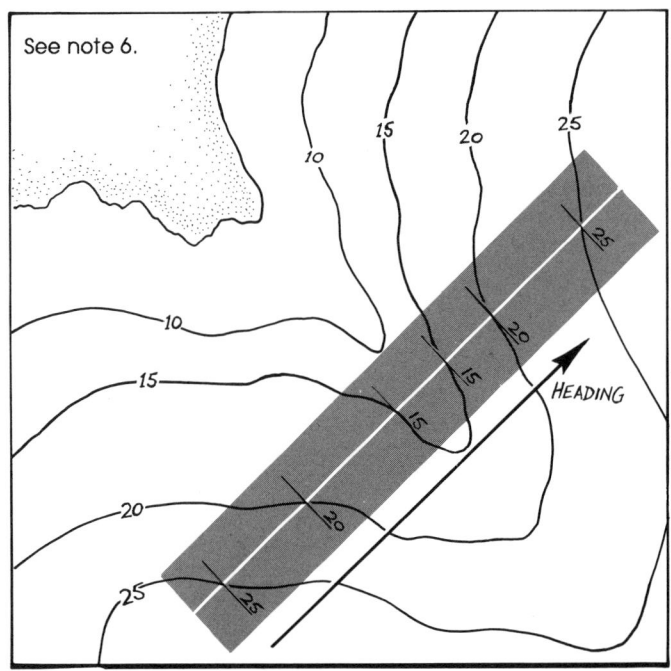

ROUNDING A HEADLAND IN FOG

Accurate DR approach, you find yourself in fog with a headland to round. Fig. 1, A is your DR plot. Give yourself a large area of uncertainty, say 8 percent instead of 5 percent of distance sailed, then take the two worst points on the circle: A_1 the most easterly and A_2 the most southerly. A, B, C would be your normal fine weather course, but if sailed from A_1 or A_2 would run you ashore. Fig. 2 shows a course $265°$, 8 miles; $223°$, 7.5 miles; $180°$ onward if sailed from A_1 or A_2 would take you clear of the headland.

Points to remember:

1. This course must be corrected for tidal direction prevailing at the time.

2. Your area of uncertainty is growing continually and if the fog does not lift you should keep off after rounding the headland.

3. At all times you will be plotting radio bearings, listening for fog signals, using your depth sounder. *Do not cut inside* your safe course unless you are certain it is safe to do so.

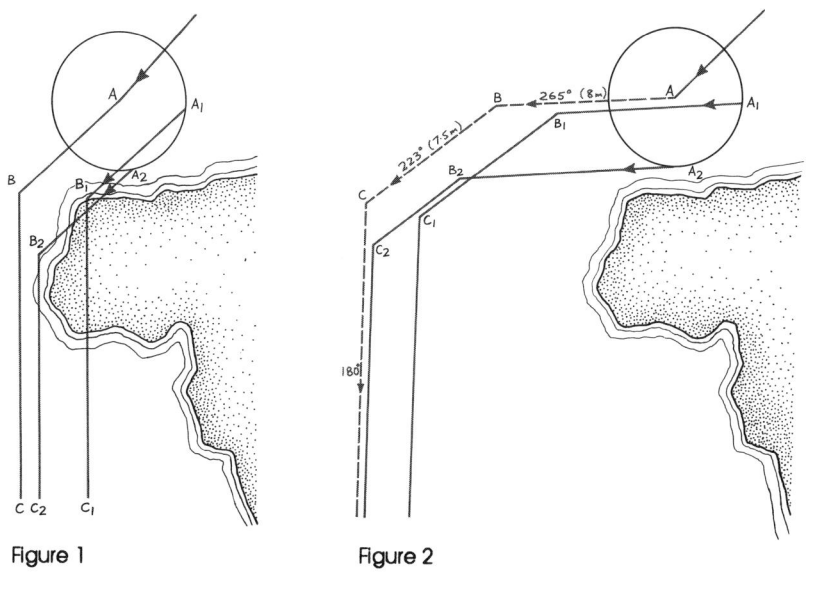

Figure 1   Figure 2

HEAVY WEATHER: Prep

❶ ASSESS SEA STATE.

❷ REDUCE SAIL OR THROTTLE BACK.

❸ BATTEN DOWN.

❹ SECURE CREW.

❺ DECIDE ON TACTICS (SEE BELOW).

1. When the weather deteriorates to a point where ship handling under reduced sail becomes difficult, when the size of the sea endangers the integrity of the ship, or when progress in a safe direction becomes near impossible, you are in danger. These three criteria are not the only ones, but they can serve as a good guide to the next set of maneuvers. All are dependent on weather fronts, winds and depressions. The size and displacement of your vessel will have some bearing upon the meeting of the above conditions. Obviously a ketch of 15 meters LOA will be able to cope with large seas with greater assurance and safety than a power vessel of 10 meters LOA. Any sound vessel, however, can undertake precautionary maneuvers to allow more or less equitable coping with bad conditions.

2. When the wind pipes up, the first thing to do is to reduce sail. However, balance is equally important, especially when reaching or beating to windward. The larger vessel will be able to hold a course longer than a small boat, due to displacement, sail-carrying ability and a larger crew. A powerboat, without the ballast or lateral plane of a sailing yacht, will have different problems to cope with. The key is to keep green water from coming aboard. Running in a powerboat demands keeping speed at one with the wave length, plowing to windward invariably demands throttling back, whilst progress in beam seas is very much a function of the dynamic stability of the hull. When the weather is truly nasty, an appropriate reduction of speed is invariably the best seamanlike judgment.

3. Everything on deck and below must be secured in heavy weather. Sails, anchors, lines, life raft, crew must be attached to the boat in a manner that precludes loss overboard. Crew especially should be in life harnesses. Anchors should be given double lashings with heavy line: a loose object of such shape and weight

Sail reduction should be planned to keep the boat moving while balancing the sail plan. Under power, speed should be adjusted to keep green water from covering the decks.

Hatch dropboards need to be secured in case of a knockdown. Any number of methods are possible, but all must be both quick to fasten and release.

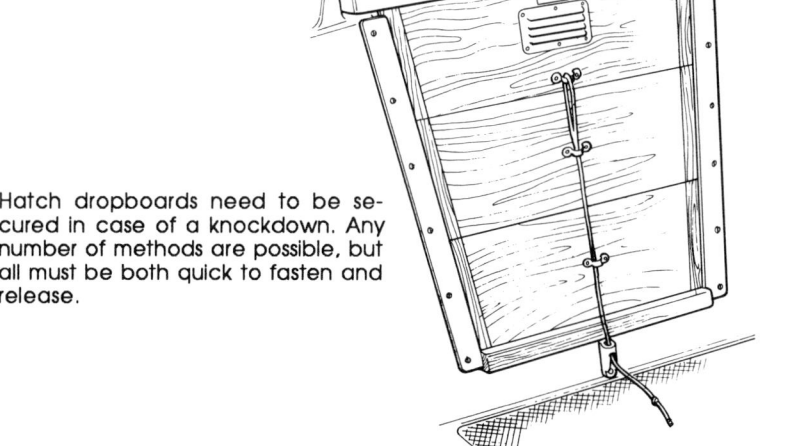

can easily hole a hull given the opportunity. Below decks, batteries have to be tied down, locker doors strong and secure–no friction or magnetic catches–books fiddled or lashed in place, stove gimbals closed, etc. Even floor boards should be able to be fastened, perhaps with button catches. In a knockdown, you will have a mess below, but any heavy object or glass or sharp implement can cause major injuries or even death. Try to avoid the worst. At the beginning of the season, it's even a good idea to tighten the engine bed fastenings. There have been cases of engines tearing loose from their mountings and causing boats to founder. Be sure to secure all hatches, ventilators, hatchboards and seacocks.

4. Much of what has been said above applies to the crew. Safety harnesses are *de rigueur* at night and in anything over a Force 5. They ought to be to government standard and constructed with two lanyards with proofed hooks/snaps. The deck attachment points must be through-bolted. Lacking such, or in emergencies, crew can lash themselves to binnacle or tracks.

5. How you will actually handle the boat in heavy weather depends to a great extent on its size, the capacity of the crew and the size of the seas and the strength of the wind. Proximity to land plays a major role in deciding tactics. In a storm, with a lee shore in sight, the inability to beat to windward and inexperienced crew, anchoring–providing the proper ground tackle is aboard–may be the only alternative. But every situation demands informed judgment–see HEAVY WEATHER: COPE.

See note 3.

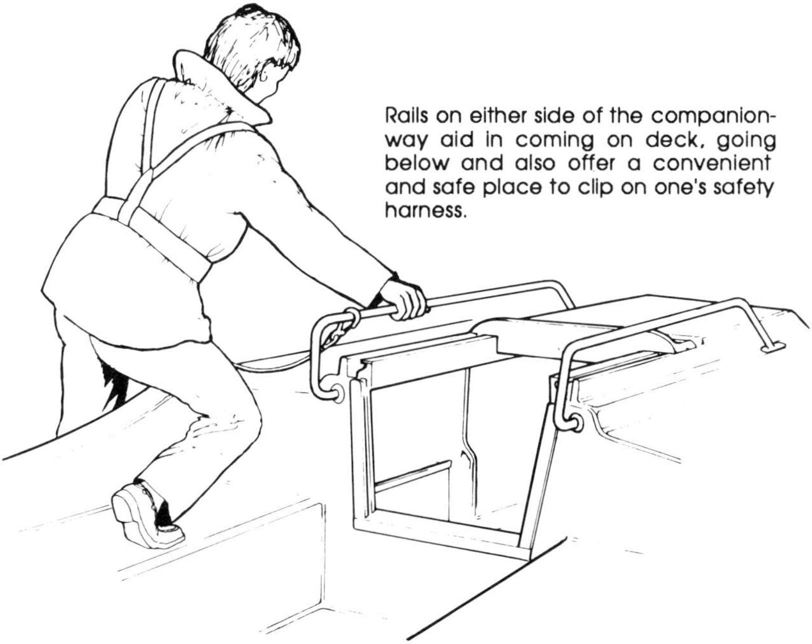

Rails on either side of the companion-way aid in coming on deck, going below and also offer a convenient and safe place to clip on one's safety harness.

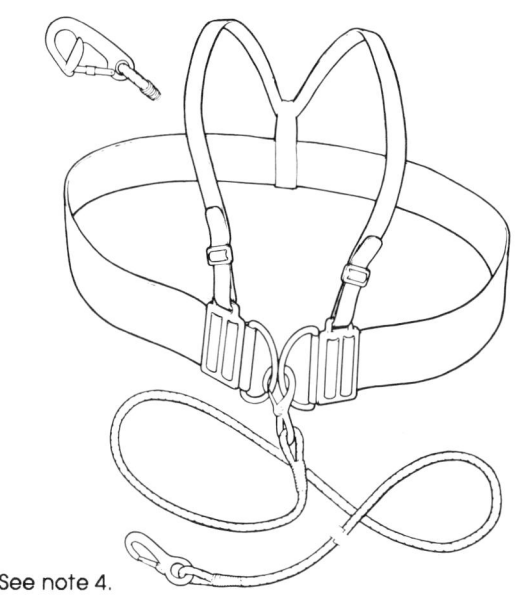

See note 4.

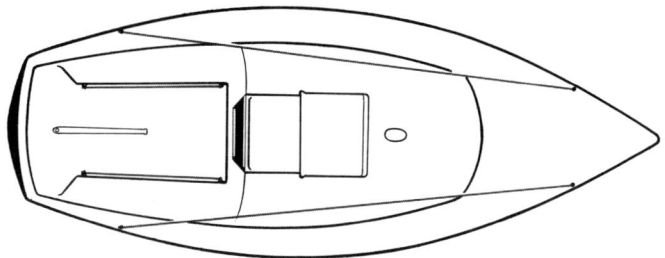

One cannot be too secure working on deck in rough seas. Harness lines, strung as shown above, allow free movement, yet do not obstruct the waterways. Clipping on to lifelines should be avoided, as one can be sprung overboard too easily.

Another good idea: string lines below, as shown, to allow one to be clipped on at that critical moment when coming on deck.

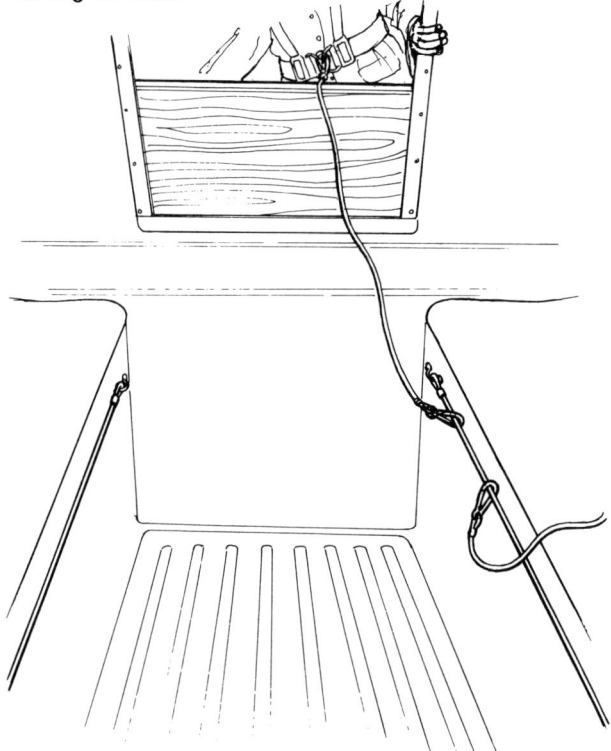

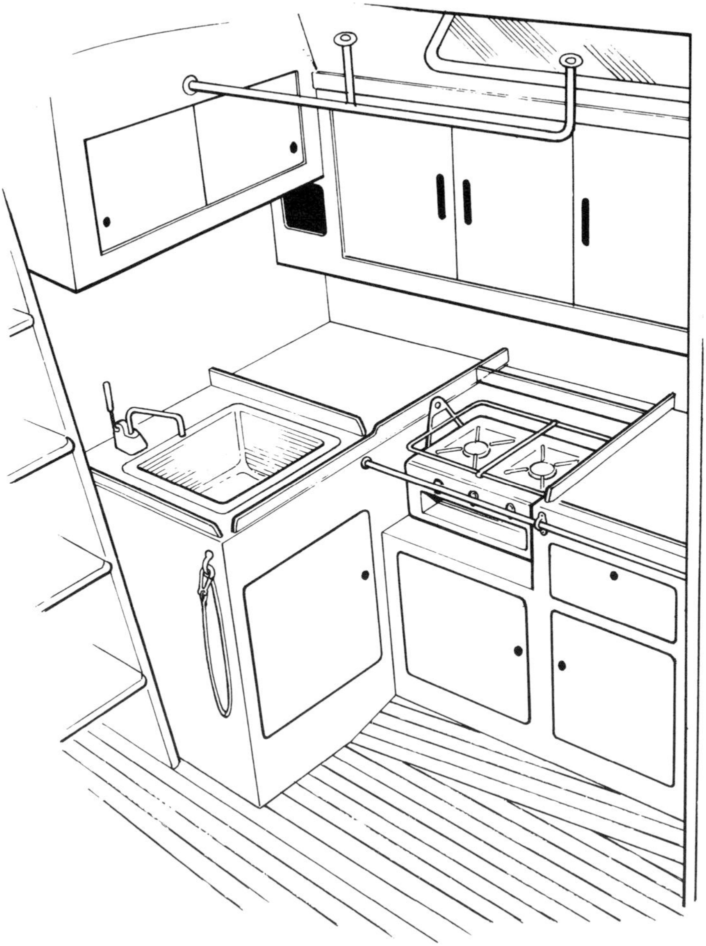

The galley is a source of grave danger from scalding, fire and heavy flying objects when the weather pipes up. Note the crash bar in front of the stove, the safety belt and the overhead rail, as well as high fiddles everywhere.

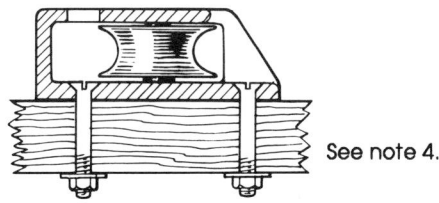

See note 4.

HEAVY WEATHER: Cope

❶ HELMSMANSHIP.

❷ SAILING TO WINDWARD.

❸ REACHING.

❹ RUNNING.

❺ LYING AHULL, HEAVING TO.

❻ SURVIVAL CONDITIONS.

1. The key man as the weather deteriorates is the helmsman. He or she needs to be fresh, alert, sensitive. He must keep a watch to windward for approaching waves, and must be alert to the need for sudden maneuvers. Keep him as protected, warm and dry as possible. When changing the guard, allow the relief to acclimatize himself to the course, conditions and "feel" of the helm before switching. A less experienced hand may require that sail be reduced to giver greater control. This is a decision the skipper must make giving due regard to approaching fronts, need to reach port, etc.

2. Sailing to windward demands not only a good eye. The necessity of pacing the boat to the height of the waves is vital. The helmsman should luff slightly as the boat comes down the face of a wave, slowing the boat and allowing the bows to rise to the oncoming crest. Otherwise there is a good chance of burying the bows and causing loss and damage to the deck gear and crew. The boat should have minimum steerage when approaching the crest of the next wave, as the speed generated surfing down the back of the wave will usually be sufficient to ascend the next one. The maneuver is one of weaving, increasing and decreasing speed offwind and upwind to keep the boat moving with a reasonable motion and as little threat to ship and crew as possible.

3. In really heavy weather, sailing in a beam sea can be courting disaster. Cresting waves can fill cockpits, cause knockdowns, or stove in a deckhouse. In less momentous seas, a tendency to broach or a difficulty in steering will probably be experienced. Either shorten sail or head off with the wind on the quarter.

See note 2.

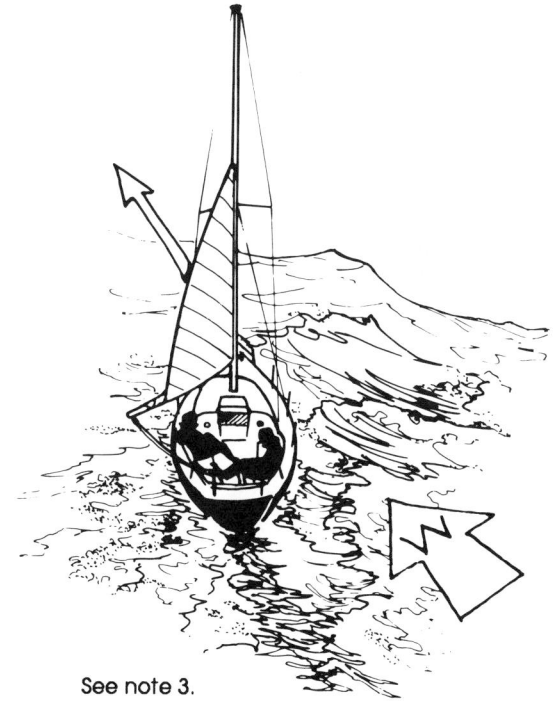

See note 3.

4. Running can be an exhilarating experience. However, when the seas build to a point where steering becomes difficult, extreme care will be needed at the helm to avoid a broach. In gale or storm conditions, don't play racer and try to carry spinnakers. Rather, reduce sail to a point where the boat is moving at optimum speed, neither in danger of surfing so fast as to be falling off the wave tops nor so slow as to lose steerage way. In mid-ocean monster storms, the need will almost always be to slow the boat down.

5. To reduce speed in severe running conditions, several methods are available. With most modern sailing vessels, the sea anchor is to be avoided. The strain it puts on the ship are greater than the advantages, and there is usually not enough forefoot to the vessel for it to keep the bows to the wind. Trailing warps does work. However, they must be many and attached so as to distribute the strains around the ship. Occassionally, anchors can be trailed from warps or bundles of chain. However, be sure to rig tripping devices or you may never get the goods aboard again. Ideally, you will let them out as needed. This does assume, however, that several hundred meters of heavy line are aboard. Oil spread overboard either from the toilet or by means of a can or bag can be effective, but very few modern yachts ever have the capacity or availability of product effectively to deploy this method of calming the seas. Also, such tactics demand a very slow-moving or still vessel. It may be most effective when lying ahull or heaving to.

6. Lying ahull is when all sail is stowed, tiller is lashed, and the ship left to look after herself. This can be a perfectly sound tactic, providing the sea room exists for leeward drift and some forward motion due to the area presented by rigging, spars and hull and tophamper. Some experiences have suggested that a shallow-hulled craft will be safer at the maneuver than a deep-draft one, as the deep keel can cause a tripping effect in certain sized seas, possibly causing a knockdown or rollover. It is also a good tactic for the singlehander in a small boat.

7. Heaving to is perhaps the simplest method of slowing a boat down and giving the crew rest in heavy going. The only maneuver required is to tack, leaving the handsail as is. Ease the main and lash the tiller to leeward. Then, depending upon adjustments of mainsheet and tiller, the boat will forereach slowly–dependent to some degree upon tophamper, sail area, keel depth, etc. The headsail should be brought in tightly before heaving to, and in heavier conditions, the main might well be dropped and secured. Of course, leeway will be made, and heaving to should not be attempted on a lee shore unless for a short time and with little sail and a deep-draft

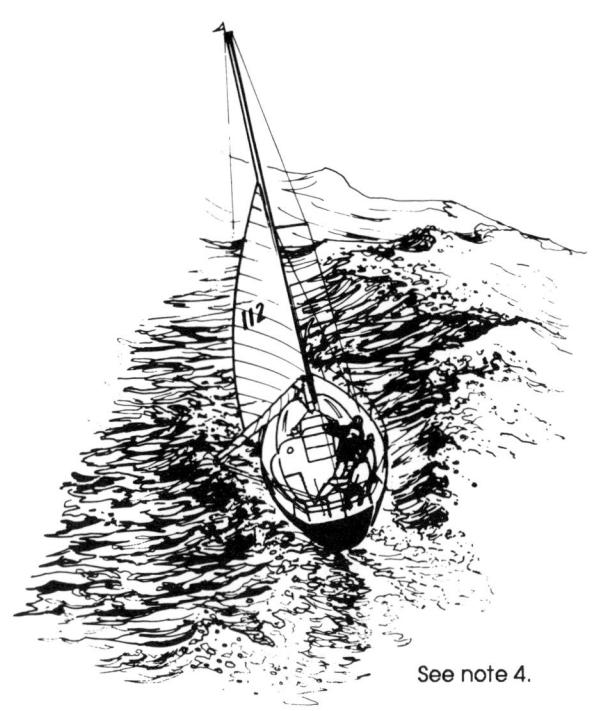

See note 4.

See note 8.

See note 5.

See note 7.

See note 6.

hull. Even then, adjustments must be made to allow for as little leeway as possible, perhaps by trimming the main to allow stronger forereaching. Chafe is always a problem when hove to; the practice is better with a working jib or storm jib than with a genoa or lapper. In very heavy going, some chafe protection around the sheet where it crosses the shrouds will not be amiss.

8. In "survival conditions," Force 10 and upward, the only possible point of sail will be running. In fact, due to the strength of the wind and severity and height of the seas, you will run no matter what. In such circumstances, it is best to rid the decks of any and all impediments that may be carried away or hamper such working of the deck as is possible. As mentioned before, oil or trailing warps is probably the best tactic. The warps should be streamed one at a time until the speed of the ship is lowered to the point where control is possible and following seas present the least threat. Extraordinary concentration at the helm is necessary and watches may be only one hour. If the lines trailed are in a bight and long enough to coincide with the seas aft, the bight may well serve to inhibit crests and smooth the attacking demons. In any storm or "ultimate" seas, stay with the boat unless it is truly foundering. Life rafts, as shown by the Fastnet disaster in 1979, are too easily flipped, drift away or cannot be entered with any degree of safety. Even with improvements–ballast pockets, drogues, heavy tether lines–chances are that you will be safer in the mother ship so long as she remains tight. Whatever, be prepared!

HOLING

❶ DO NOT PANIC!

❷ LOCATE THE HOLE IMMEDIATELY.

❸ SEAL THE OPENING WITH MATERIALS AT HAND.

❹ IF FAR FROM PORT, CONSIDER PERMANENT REPAIRS.

1. If you strike an object, immediately go below and check for damage. If a hole has been rent in the hull near the waterline, sail on the tack to keep the hole above water.

2. More than likely, the hole will be hidden behind bunks or lockers or beneath immovable floorboards. There is only one solution:

Tear the furniture out! It hurts, but failure to do so immediately will result in probable foundering. Using a pry bar or axe or large spanner, wrench the offending woodwork (or glasswork) away.

3. Use either an umbrella patch or cushions stuffed into or against the hole to stop the major flow. Another interesting possibility is to use a plumber's helper over the hole, preferably from the outside. If the hole is well below the waterline, the inflow of water will be close to twice as fast as higher up, and may be much harder to reach. The storm jib, with lines at each corner, can be passed around the hull from outside to form a patch. Reduce the speed of the vessel to allow the sail to stay in position. Weight the corner with chain or odd fitments shackled together to allow it to sink below the water. No matter how hard and fast you work, a lot of water will enter the ship. The average bilge pump–25 gallons per minute–will be next to useless when up against a flow of over 200 gallons per minute, which is what you can expect from a hole about 4 inches in diameter. Only a high-capacity engine-driven pump can handle a flow like that, and then only if the engine has not been flooded. A bucket brigade can be of help, but the key is speed in locating the hole and speed and efficiency in stemming the flow.

4. Once the flow is stopped, or slowed to a leak, more permanent repairs can be effected. Perhaps the best material, in anything but a wood boat, is underwater-hardening epoxy paste. Follow directions, but do try to apply it on the outside first with some sort of temporary board or backing held in place. Then apply to the interior. Remember to spread the paste well past the area of the hole to allow for good surface adhesion. In a wooden ship, boards and caulking can be used to first seal the opening from within, with further repairs made from the outside as conditions allow.

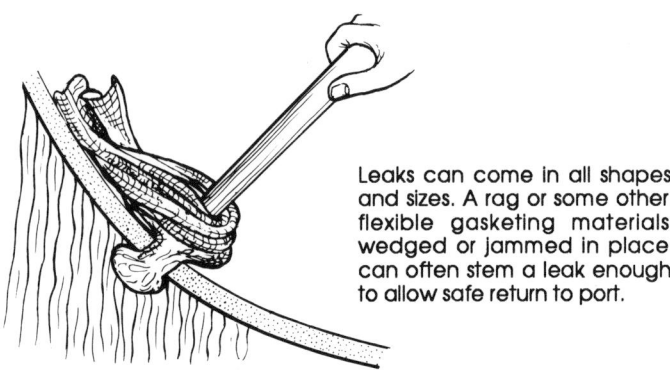

Leaks can come in all shapes and sizes. A rag or some other flexible gasketing materials wedged or jammed in place can often stem a leak enough to allow safe return to port.

ICING

❶ SLOW THE SHIP DOWN.

❷ IF THE CONDITIONS PERMIT, RUN DOWNWIND.

❸ PREPARE TO SEND A MAN ALOFT WITH TOOLS.

❹ IF POSSIBLE, REDUCE SAIL AND POWER.

1. Ice will increase the topside weight, reducing stability and the righting moment of any ship. Slowing the vessel will permit gentler motion and more time to remedy the condition.

2. Since a sailing vessel is generally more stable when running, there will be less chance of capsizing and an easier motion to work aloft. Keep up only enough sail to reduce rolling.

3. The only way to remove ice from the rigging is to hack it off with a mallet or the dull side of a small axe. Other than the deck man handling the bosun's chair, no one else should be on deck, as falling ice can inflict serious injury.

4. If conditions permit, keep up only a patch of sail to reduce rolling and power until the ice has been removed. Under any icing conditions, seek refuge as soon as possible. Not only is the ship in danger, but the crew can suffer from hypothermia and frostbite.

When someone must go aloft to break away ice, be sure that both that person and the crew member handling the halyard below are well padded. Falling ice can inflict serious injury.

JURY RIGS: Masts

❶ ASSESS THE DAMAGE.

❷ MAKE AN INVENTORY OF AVAILABLE PARTS, BROKEN AND OTHERWISE.

❸ DESIGN THE NEW RIG.

❹ ASSEMBLE THE PARTS ON DECK.

❺ RAISE THE JURY RIG.

❻ SET SAIL.

1. Depending upon the damage inflicted to the mast (see DISMASTING), a jury rig may be an addition to what remains standing, or it may be an entire make-do structure. If the mast has broken above the spreaders, the storm trysail may work as a mainsail with only a forestay and backstay pieced together from spare wire and wire rope clips. If only the mizzen remains, a forestay can be fashioned–albeit at a very low angle–and a jib can be modified to be set flying from said stay. As long as the remaining bit of mast has retained the lower shrouds, a low efficient sailing rig is not only possible but relatively simple to fabricate.

2. If the mast breaks at or near deck level, a different set of criteria apply. First, see what is salvageable from the leavings of your once noble spar. It may be possible to save stays, hardware or a section of the spar itself. Before you decide what you will do, see what you have to work with.

3. Having made an inventory of working materials–not forgetting oars, spinnaker and jockey poles, bunk fronts, etc.–sit below with a clean sheet of paper, some basic measurements (base of fore triangle, length of longest usable mast section, length of various salvaged wire, etc.) and a pencil and see what *might* be possible–what L. Francis Herreshoff called "thought experiments." It will be much easier than trying different combinations on deck in a seaway at night with the wind at Force 6. Perhaps the most important thing to remember is that the rig you design must be able to be created, hoisted and used by the available manpower and the available skills. If you are within sight of land, turn on the engine! However, if you are mid-ocean you will want to devise something that will take you

Some sort of spar held aloft is necessary for a jury rig. Try to think creatively about the possibilities. Usually storm sails or foresail can be best rigged to provide a more-or-less efficient propulsive device.

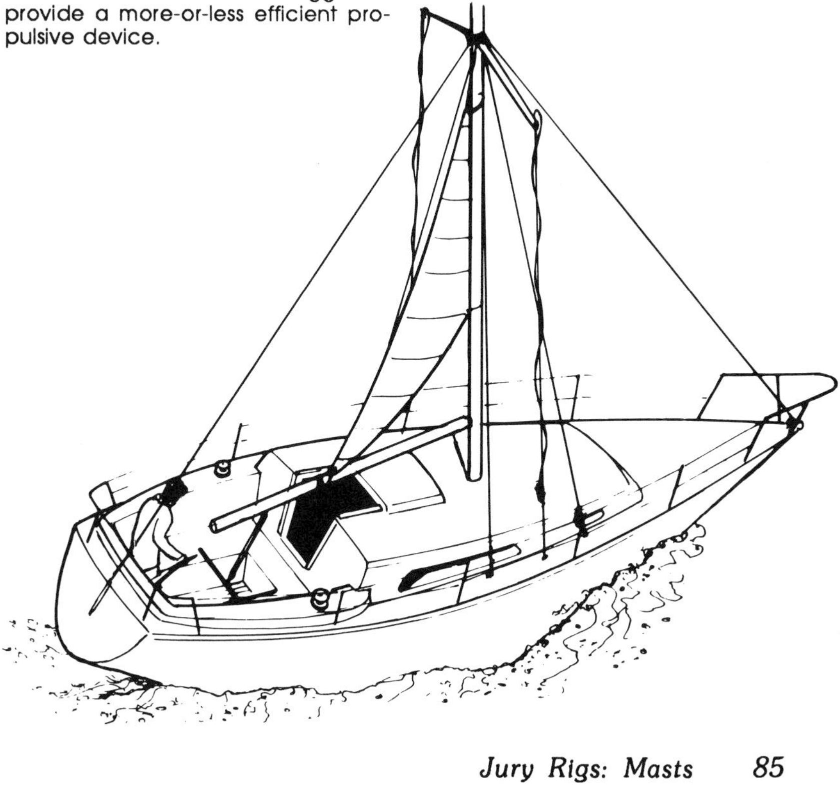

where you want to go with the available rations and water aboard in whatever weather you may reasonably expect to have.

4. Having decided on the solution, gather the crew, explain the jury rig to them and delegate one crew member to each task needed to raise the rig. Collect and assemble all the necessary parts. Do as much as possible with the new rig *on deck*. The less you need to do aloft, the safer. Make sure, for example, that all the "masthead" fittings are secured, that the correct length wires and ropes are tied off. You don't want to have to lower the whole mess if you can avoid it.

5. Depending on size and weight, raising the rig can be a job for one with a winch and a triprod arrangement or it can take the muscles of ten strong men. You wish to get the thing up with minimal effort. The illustrations give some possible solutions.

6. Setting sail may mean adopting some odd and back-ended configurations. Jibs may be turned on end, or sewn together. Storm sails may be the best driving sails for a reduced rig, and setting them flying may be the best, and safest, means of propulsion. What is most important is to devise a sail combination that will get you where you wish to go. Quite often sprit sails, lateen rigs, makeshift schooners and squaresails will serve the purpose quite well if you know anything about them. Unfortunately, the modern sailor has little use for working sails of the past. The illustrations demonstrate their uses.

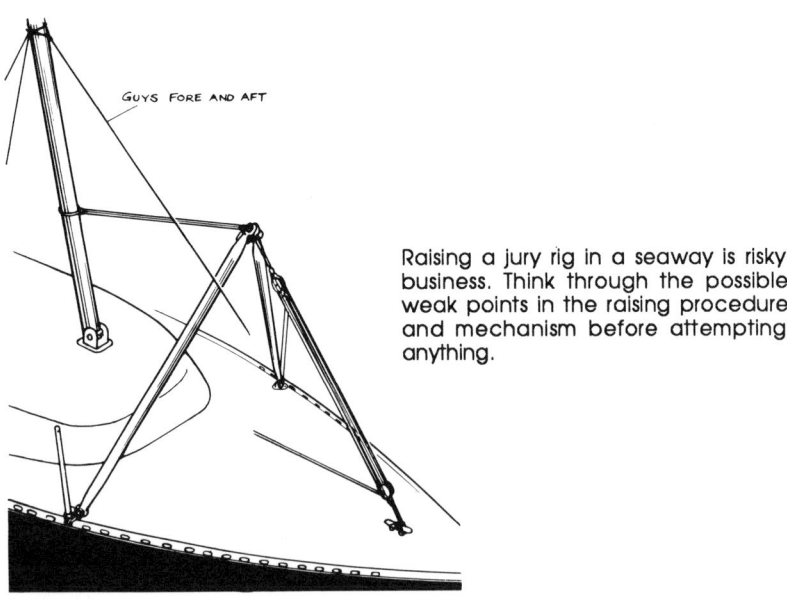

GUYS FORE AND AFT

Raising a jury rig in a seaway is risky business. Think through the possible weak points in the raising procedure and mechanism before attempting anything.

See note 6.

JURY RIGS: *Rudders*

❶ DETERMINE HOW THE RUDDER IS DAMAGED.

❷ IF ONLY TILLER, SEE TILLER: BREAKAGE.

❸ IF STEERING GEAR IS UNREPAIRABLE, SEE BELOW.

❹ REPAIRS ARE DIFFERENT FOR OUTBOARD AND INBOARD RUDDERS.

1. If the rudder is inboard and the stock has been bent, ingnore it. Instead, you will have to fashion a rudder of sweep to work off the transom. If the blade is damaged, it may still be possible to steer the boat, albeit with reduced sail. However, if the response is minimal and you are still some distance from port, some sort of jury-rigged rudder will have to be constructed.

2. Should the steering gear be damaged beyond repair, an emergency tiller should be aboard. Since many more yachts are wheel-steered now than even twenty years ago, essential spares should be carried–cable, clamps, sprocket wheels, gears, etc. Obviously, you will never be covered for all contingencies. And, sooner or later, you will have to rig that emergency tiller. Accidents do happen that will incapacitate both wheel and rudder.

3. The simplest repairs are to a transom-hung rudder, which can be shipped and patched, or even replaced from parts fashioned from floorboards, hatchboards, etc. If the pintles and gudgeons are not bent or broken, repairs should be fairly straightforward, and if the rudder is wood, can be accommodated with screws and bolts. If the rudder is fiberglass, the same methods can be used but reinforcement will be necessary in the form of load-spreading washers (of metal or wood) and lashings. However, if the major portion of the blade has been torn away, and the fastenings between rudder and hull are left without integrity, a new rudder assembly will have to be fashioned.

4. Inboard rudders pose a different set of problems. If the rudder bearing has been broken, and the rudder is slamming back and forth, potential exists for major hull damage or rupture, especially in a seaway. Some means of locking the rudder in position, or even of shipping the entire assembly, will have to be devised. One good precaution is to drill a small hole in the trailing edge of the blade,

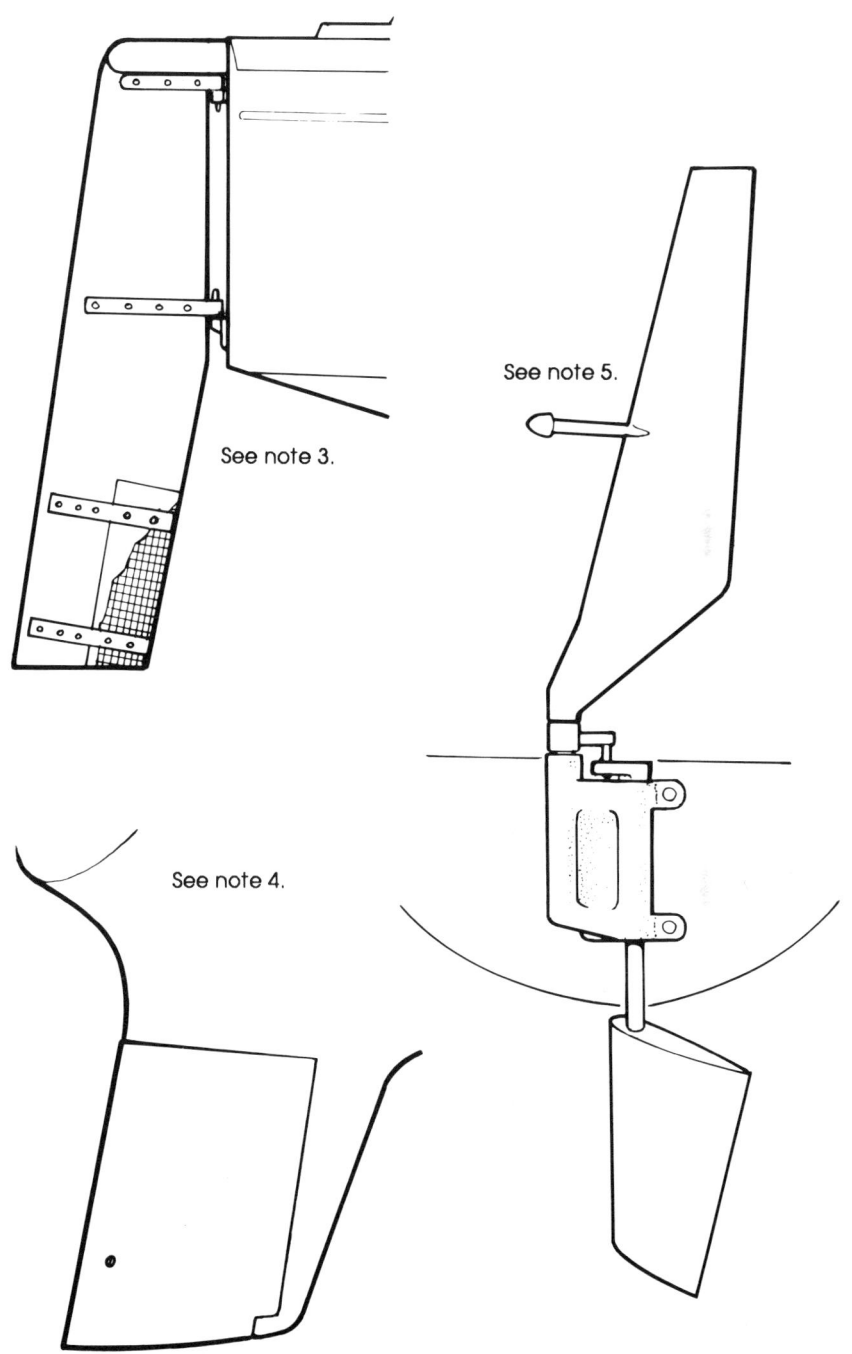

See note 3.

See note 5.

See note 4.

with the foreknowledge that this will be used, should an emergency occur, to lead lines outboard and to the cockpit for steering. If the blade can be set, a rudder aft will still have to be fashioned.

5. Some self-steering wind vanes can be adapted to act as an auxiliary rudder. This potential might well be investigated when contemplating the purchase of a vane.

6. To actually construct a new rudder, first gather the necessary materials: a pole–boom, spinnaker pole, oar (if long enough); a blade substitute such as a hatchboard or section of floorboard; line, lashings, bolts, tools needed, etc. Fasten the pole to the blade with through bolts, U-bolts, or anything that will produce a rigid structure. Next, determine how to attach the assembly to the stern. As long as the blade will be deeply immersed, any method will do. However, stern shape will determine the most appropriate way of accomplishing this.

7. Perhaps the easiest stern to mount your new rudder will be virtually plumb, utilizing the pushpit horizontals as fastening points, with stout lashings to hold the two together. Reverse-counter transoms will demand a more deck-level approach with some fitting being used to hold the lashing. Traditional forward-sloping counters will best use the pushpit as above. Lacking guard rails aft, deck-level sashings will have to be used, remembering that with a single-point lashing some means will have to be devised to hold the blade in the water. Ballasting is one possibility. Another is to run lines from a hold in the *forward* edge of the blade near the bottom, outboard and forward to strong points on deck. The backstay can also be used as a second lashing point for the pole/stock, remembering that any lashing used here will put enormous strains on the entire rig and should be used advisedly in heavy weather.

8. To ease steering, lines can be led through snatch blocks attached to the pushpit at either outboard corner, or a spar can be slashed to the pushpit, or deck and blocks can be attached to either end, in either case with lines leading from the new rudder "stock" through the blocks and thence to winches or cleats in the cockpit.

9. Despite advice to the contrary, it is always better to attempt to fix the tiller at the centerline. Even without a pushpit, some makeshift arrangement can be worked out on the afterdeck, usually by lashing a spar to the mooring cleats at the quarters and affixing the rudder stock to the spar.

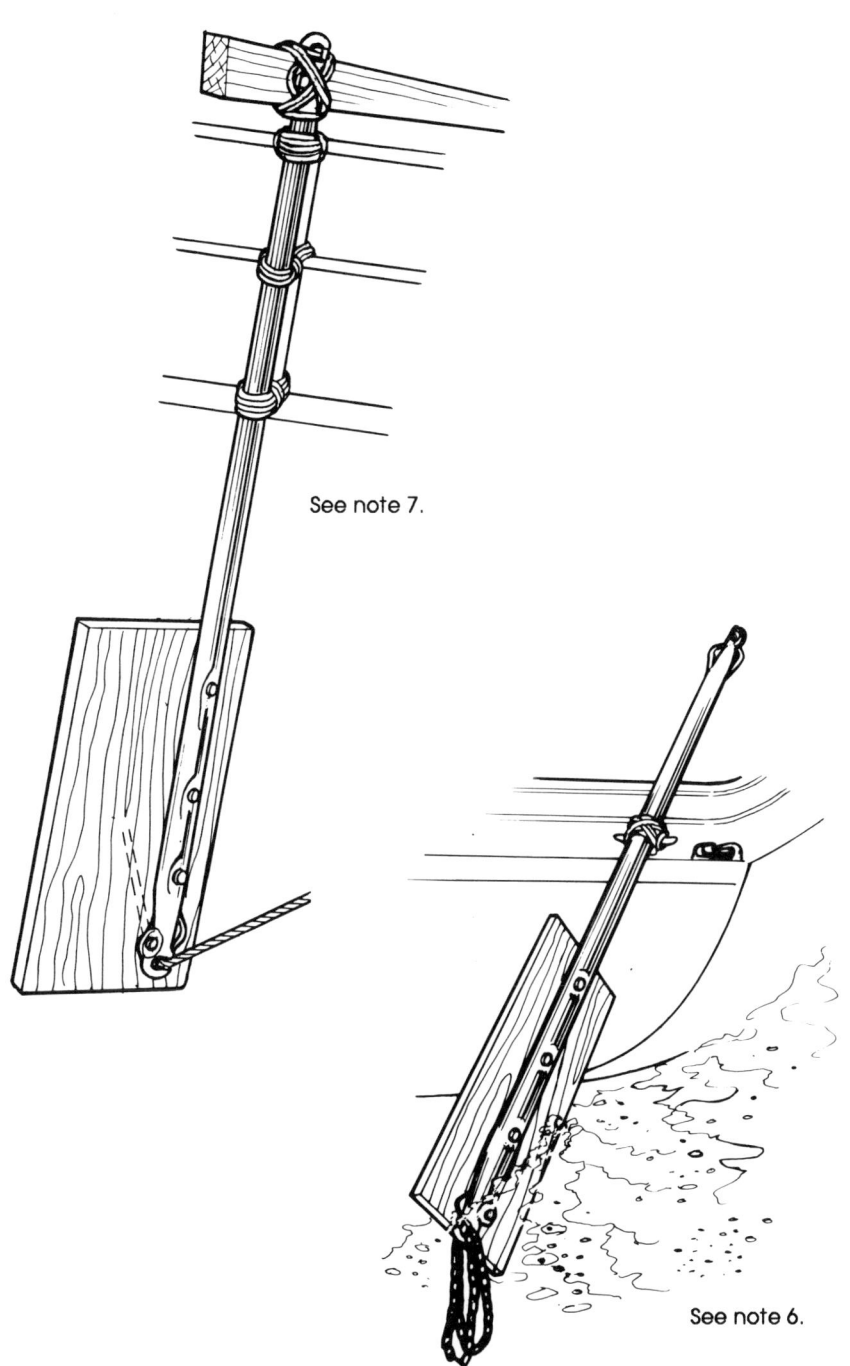

See note 7.

See note 6.

10. A drogue can be utilized for steering–tire, bucket or proper drogue–with steering lines attached to the drogue line with rolling hitches. To give the needed steering leverage, the ends of the steering lines should be led through blocks on either end of a fairly long spar lashed to the stern. Be sure to rig a tripping line for the drogue. You will find recovery difficult otherwise. Also, this arrangement, although the easiest to rig, will not offer the control of a jury rudder.

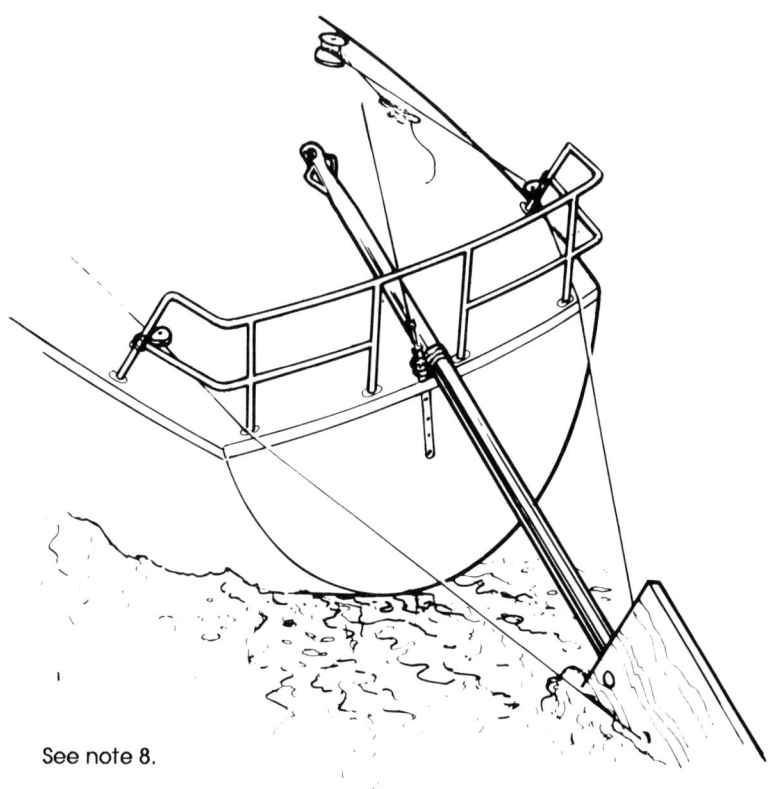

See note 8.

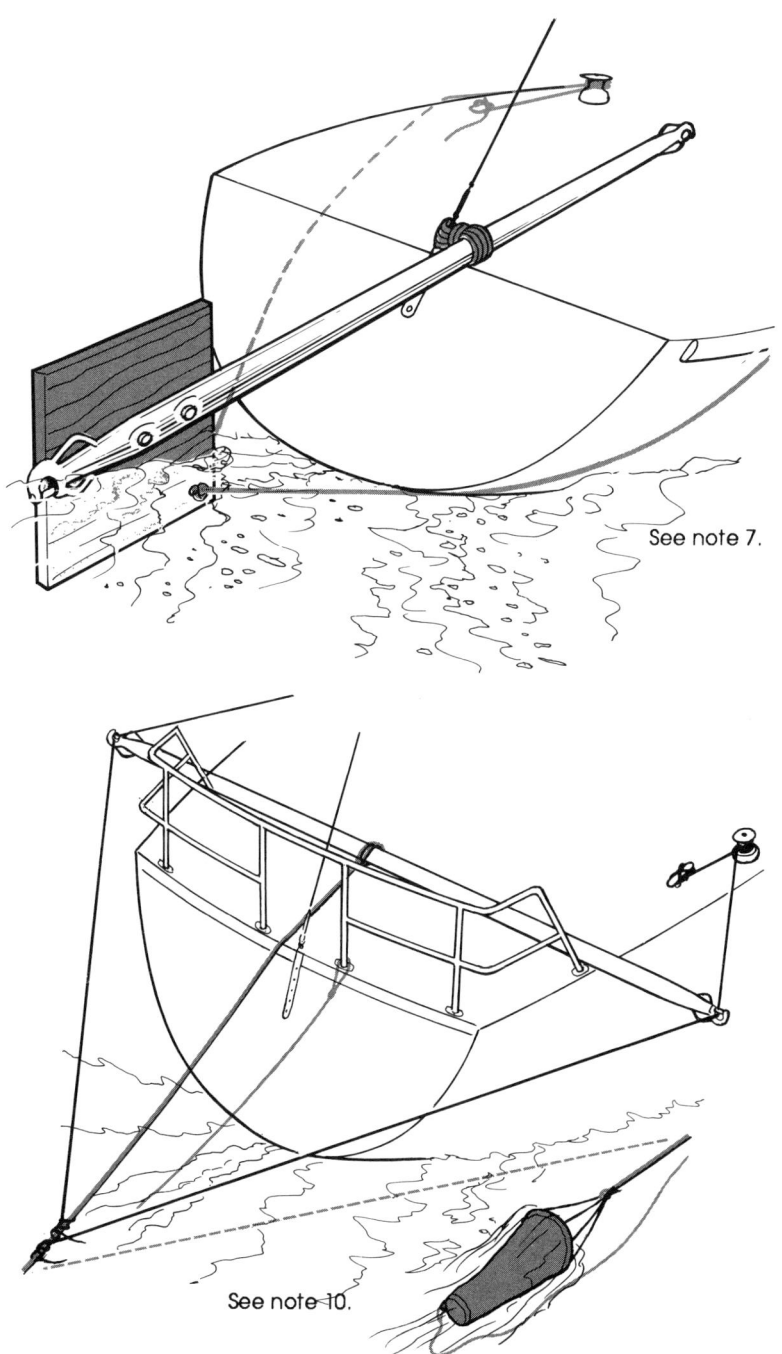

See note 7.

See note 10.

LEAKS

❶ LOCATE THE LEAK.

❷ IF POSSIBLE, ISOLATE.

❸ REPAIR.

1. Locating a leak may be much more difficult than you might imagine. Likely spots are seacocks, rudder gland, stuffing box, keelbolts, hull-to-deck join, deck fittings–in fact anywhere the hull or deck has been drilled, cut or opened to receive a fitting, including water, waste or fuel tanks. Too often, the leak is far from the spot at which water, etc., collects. You may have to trace the course.

2. A deck leak may be uncomfortable, but a hull leak, fitting or otherwise (skegs and keel sumps can crack from wracking strains in heavy seas), can be downright dangerous. Though the pumps may be able to cope, track it down. And don't forget the obvious: head intake hoses are usually not looped high enough. At rest this may be unnoticeable, but underway, especially when heeled, the head can overflow and cause a boat to founder. If the boat has sealed-off compartments, or if an area can be sealed off by makeshift means, do so until repairs can be safely effected.

3. Attempt to stop the leak with rags, caulking cotton, foam or neoprene or plugs. (Incidentally, all through hulls, even those with seacocks, should have a tapered softwood plug of appropriate size tied to the fitting with a lanyard.) Rubber and silicon caulking will *not* hold to wet surfaces. Underwater epoxy will, and should be kept aboard for such emergencies.

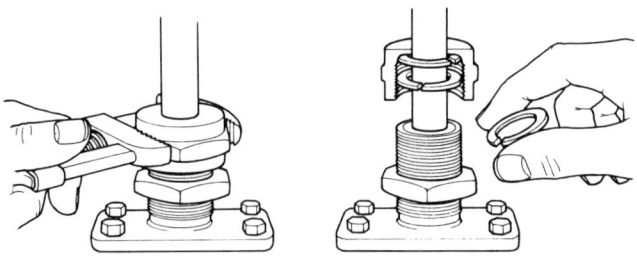

Stuffing boxes are prime candidates for leaks. Make sure all clamps are tightened, packing is secure and the lock nut is neither loose nor cracked.

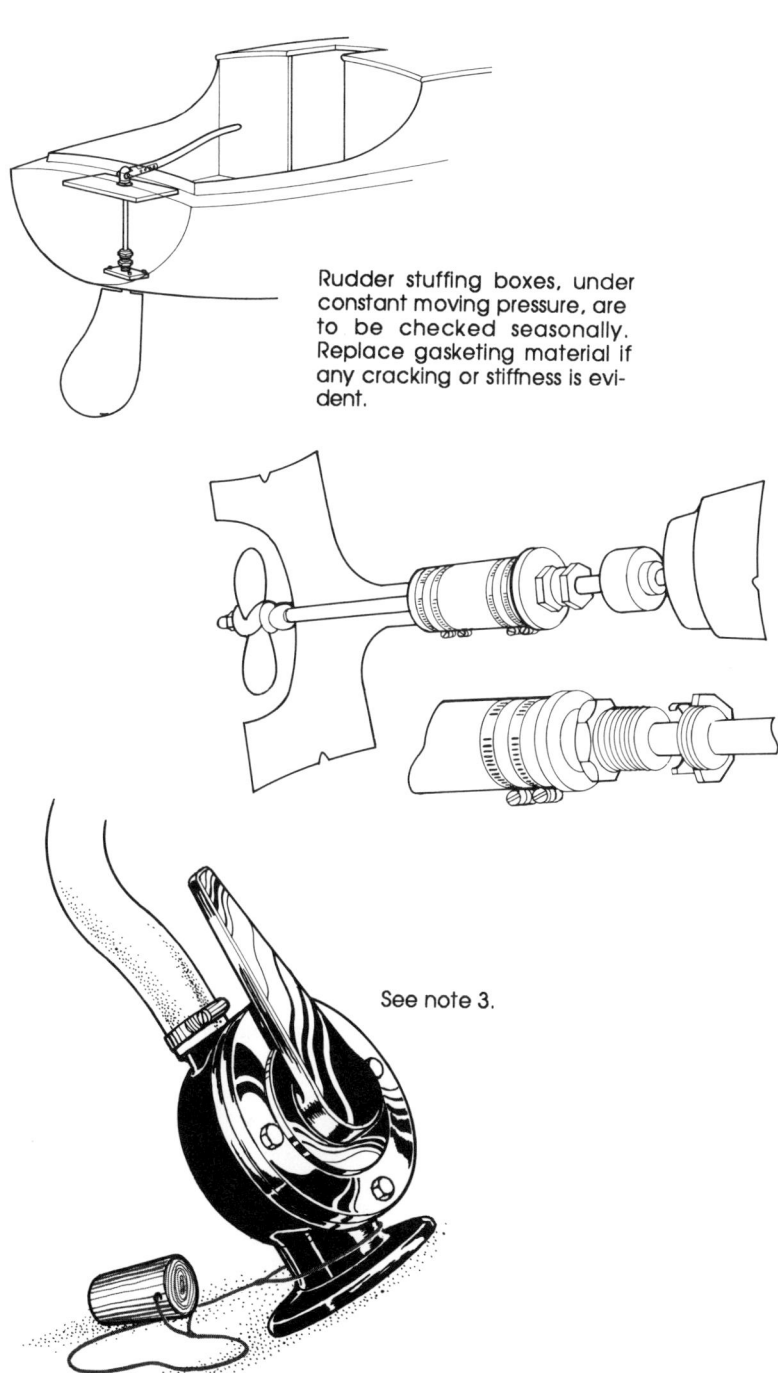

Rudder stuffing boxes, under constant moving pressure, are to be checked seasonally. Replace gasketing material if any cracking or stiffness is evident.

See note 3.

LEE SHORES

❶ LAY OUT A SECOND ANCHOR IN THE DINGHY.

❷ HOIST SAILS AND LET THEM RUN FREE.

❸ CARRY THE SECOND ANCHOR AFT AND SECURE IT TO A STERN CLEAT.

❹ BRING UP THE STERN WARP SO THAT THE BOAT IS BEAM-ON THE WIND.

❺ RAISE THE BOW ANCHOR.

❻ BUOY THE STERN WARP AND LET GO.

❼ SAIL OUT TO WINDWARD.

1. Under most conditions a lee shore should be avoided only because of the possibility of heavy weather. If no choice exists, try to anchor as far out as is possible with safety.

2. If the engine is powerful, motor sailing should be attempted before trying to leave under sail alone.

3. In truly horrendous conditions, boats have survived by sailing in a half-circle and dropping as many anchors as are on board. Under these conditions it will not be possible to set anything from the dinghy and no other choice will exist.

4. Careful planning and coordination from all the crew will be necessary for these maneuvers to work. It will be difficult to keep the headsail from flogging itself to death and the jib sheets from fouling. However, your safety depends on this, and a crew member should be stationed at what will be the leeward winch to haul in as soon as the anchor line has been released. Another must be stationed at the mainsheet, leaving the helmsman free to concentrate.

5. When alone or shorthanded, it may be an advantage to sail the yacht out under only one sail, whichever is most efficient, keeping the decks relatively clear. If you must lose an anchor, do so...it costs less than the ship.

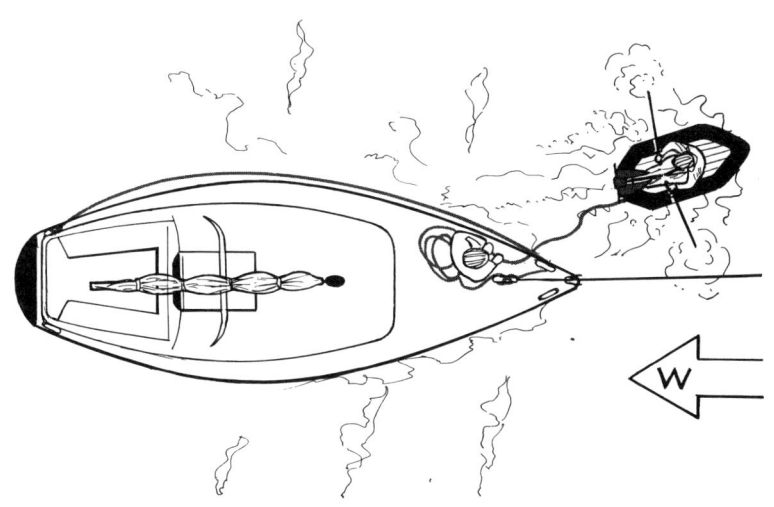

See note 2.

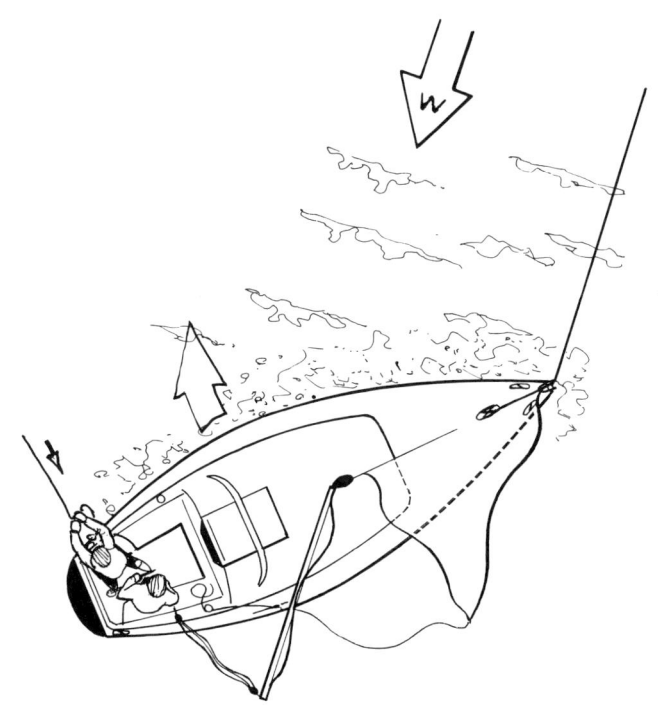

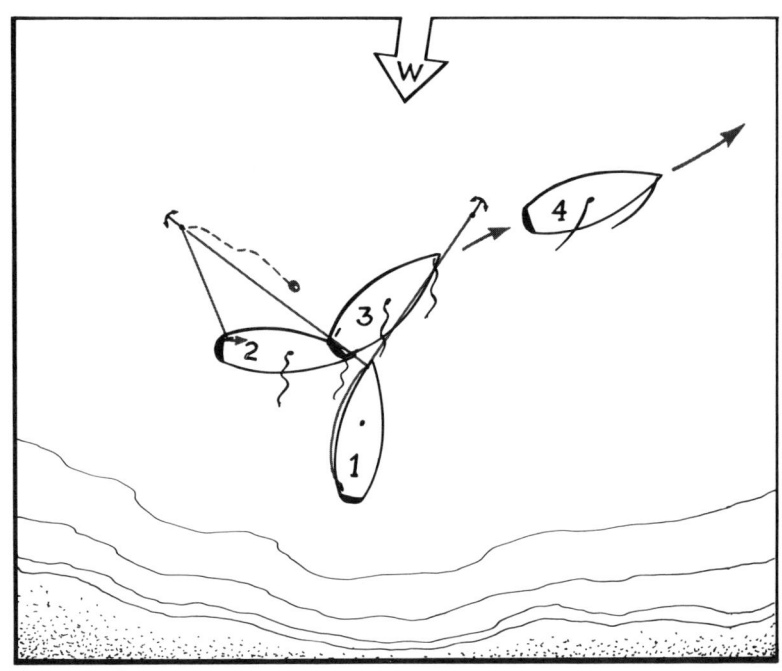

See note 3.

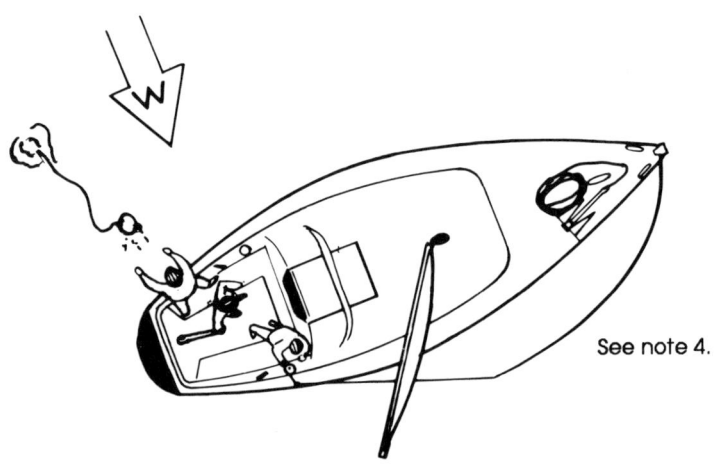

See note 4.

LIFE RAFTS

❶ KEEP ON DECK.

❷ USE A FASTENING SYSTEM THAT ALLOWS QUICK RELEASE, EITHER PATENT OR PROPER LASHINGS.

❸ KEEP SERVICED.

❹ INSTRUCT THE CREW IN PROPER USAGE.

❺ TIE THE PAINTER TO A STRONG POINT ON DECK.

❻ INFLATE BY GIVING THE PAINTER A SHARP JERK.

❼ DO NOT CUT PAINTER UNTIL ALL ARE ABOARD THE RAFT.

1. It should be obvious that a life raft must be kept on deck or in a special raft locker. Nevertheless, many yachtsmen place it in a cockpit or lazarette locker where accumulations of gear and debris block access to it. Under-the-sole lockers are not recommended; too many people will be in the cockpit to make for easy access. The best location is either lashed to the coachroof fore or aft or the mast, or on the afterdeck or beneath the helmsman seat. Some newer boats have special recesses within the transom; these are fine if, in practice, you can get to them without endangering the crew. Best to keep all safety gear inboard if possible.

2. Don't use lashings that end up like the Gordian knot. They must be slashable with one stroke of a knife, or with a single tug on a line–some variant of a slippery hitch, for example. The lashings are best done up on natural cordage, as synthetics will slip too much. Manila or hemp–if you can find them–are good. Patent hold-down systems can be acceptable, providing they are constantly checked for corrosion or chafe. Like anything mechanical they are liable to seizure and breakdown when most needed.

3. Servicing is vital to life raft performance. Kept on deck, the raft, even in a fiberglass cannister, is subject to moisture penetration, fabric deterioration and valve failure. Yearly servicing by an authorized service center is vital. Yes, it is expensive. Yes, you need to do it. While we are on the subject, do buy a cannister raft. Valises are too subject to kicks, seepage and puncture. They should be avoided at all costs, no matter how well-protected you believe the

raft to be. Also, pay a few dollars or pounds more and get a raft that is up to SOLAS standards. The difference, especially offshore, is worth it both in terms of construction and materials specifications and in terms of equipment.

4. The crew, every member of it, must be given proper instruction in abandon-ship and life-raft drill. Don't wait until it is too late. This is not to suggest you should inflate the raft to practice, but do use the dinghy to get the crew used to boarding a raft in rough seas and in a state of mock panic, something best done at one's moorings. Show them how to undo lashings, how to toss the raft overboard and how to inflate it. Make sure, when underway, that each crew member is supplied with a sharp and properly protected knife.

5. Depending where the raft is located, the painter should be tied to a deck fitting which is *through-bolted*. The strains upon raft and painter in rough seas when thrown are great. Stanchion bases, mast step, coachroof rails, pushpit are all appropriate.

6. *Never attempt to inflate the raft while it is on board!* What with rigging, deck gear, trampling crew, wheel or tiller, etc., you will never be able to get into the water, and if you do, the chances are you will rip the fabric or tear off a fitting or two. Always throw it clear of the ship. The painter can become tangled. First make sure it is clear, then tug firmly. The throw of the raft may start inflation, but it is always best to make sure by giving the painter the approved and appropriate pull. If the raft does not inflate, or only partially fills, get one person to attempt to start pumping. Make sure that individual is secure in a safety harness.

7. Should abandonment of the mother vessel become imperative, make sure *all* members of the crew are aboard the raft before cutting the painter. Rafts drift–especially in the conditions likely at the time–at a remarkable rate. There is little or no chance that contact can be reestablished with the yacht. As tragic experience has unfortunately shown, all too often, in panic, some crew member cuts that figurative umbilical cord prematurely. Someone is sure to be the worse for it.

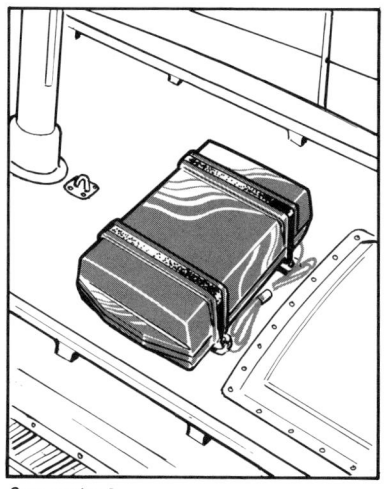

See note 1.

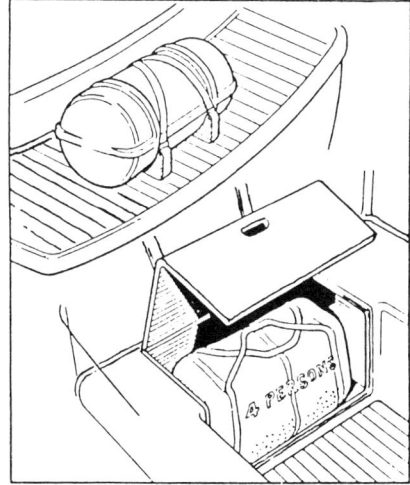

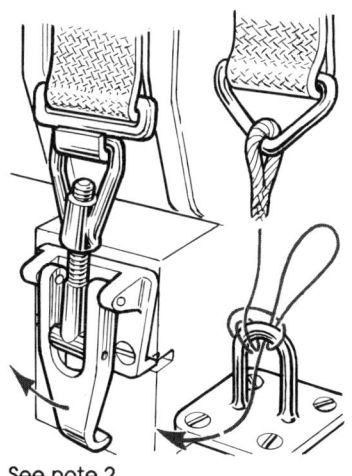

See note 2.

See note 5.

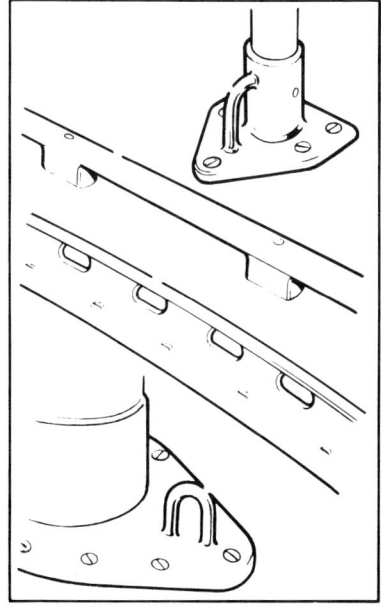

Life Rafts 101

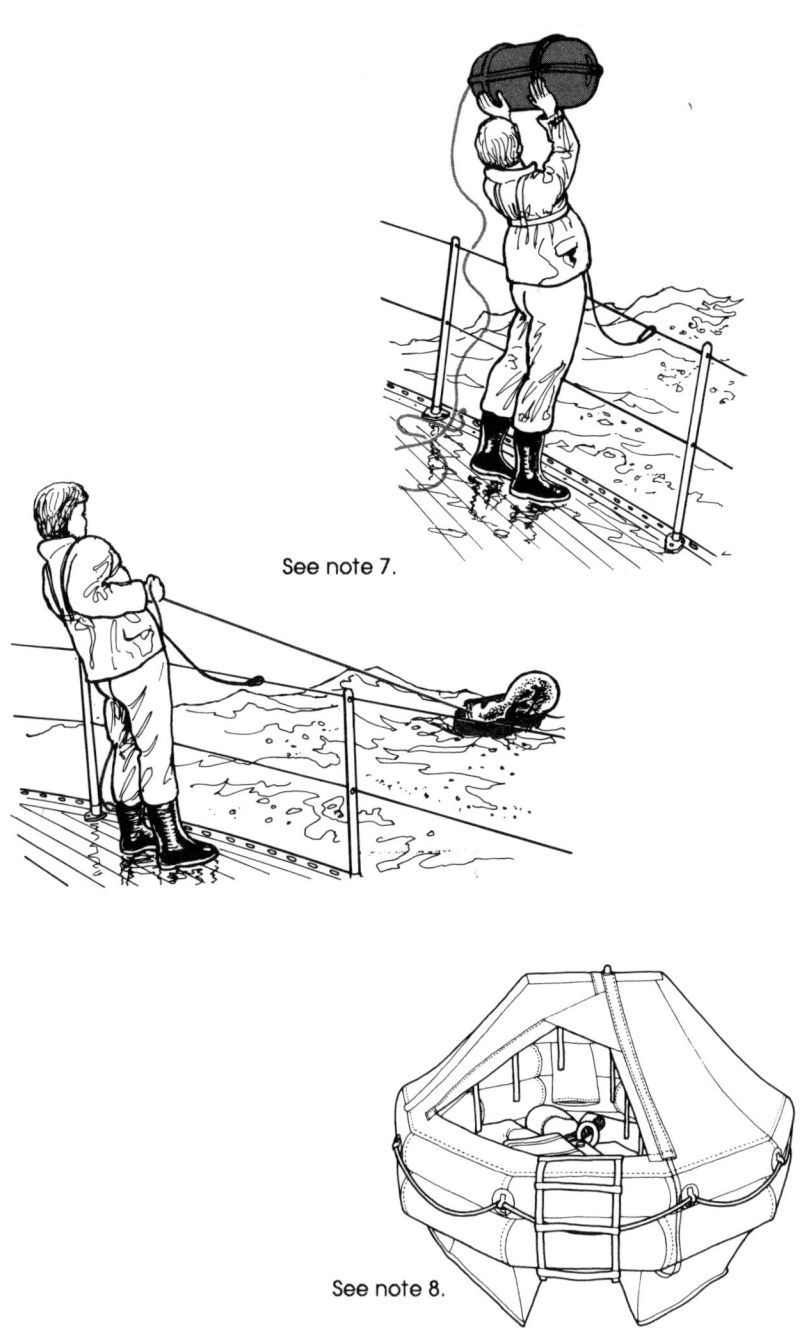

See note 7.

See note 8.

LIGHTNING

❶ IN AN ELECTRICAL STORM, GET CREW BELOW.

❷ STAY WELL AWAY FROM ANY METAL FITTINGS.

❸ IF CONDITIONS PERMIT THE SHIP TO BE ANCHORED OR HOVE TO, DO IT.

1. Lightning is always unpredictable. Though it will rarely strike a yacht enough cases exist, especially along the American eastern seaboard, to take all possible precautions. Since lightning will follow the most direct path to the water, it is up to you to provide such a path to help it on its way.

2. Though copper wire #8 is generally recommended for a lightning ground, much better is to use copper tubing, flattened at the ends connecting the lightning rod at the masthead with a keel bolt in a boat with an encapsulated keel, a grounding plate should be attached to the hull as far below the waterline as is feasible.

3. Because very few European boats are fitted with lightning protection, in a sudden storm a length of chain, shackled to the cap shroud and dangled overboard (make sure it is long enough to remain under water) will act as a satisfactory substitute. If time exists, tape the shackle end of the chain to the shroud to ensure positive contact.

4. Obviously, the helmsman remains in greater danger than the rest of the crew, especially if steering with a wheel. If possible, anchor; when at sea, heave to and join the rest of the crew below.

Any grounding wire or tube should be secured to the grounding plate with tightened nuts of conductive material.

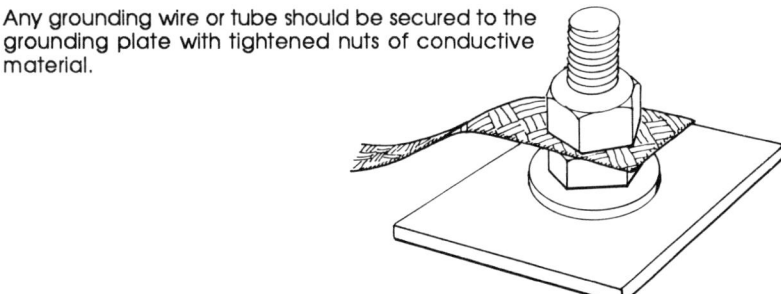

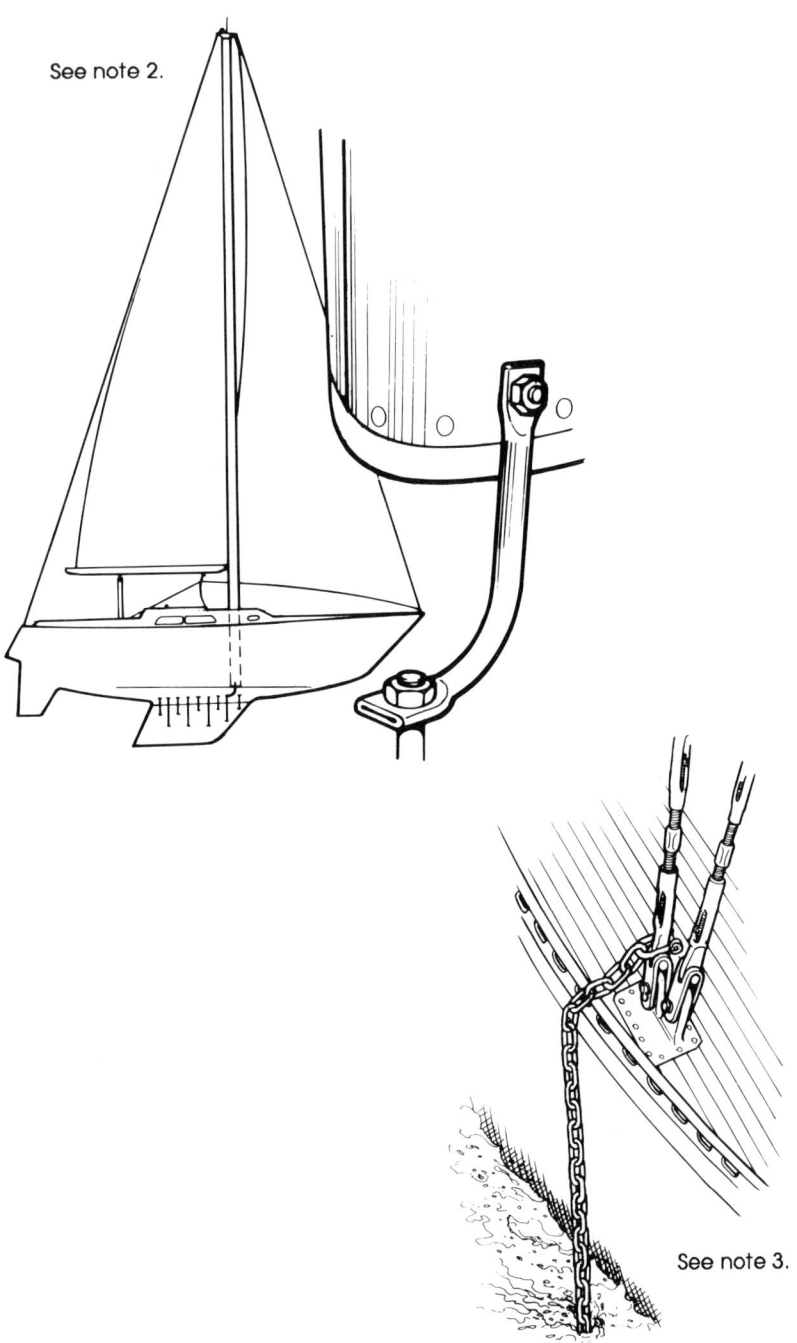

See note 2.

See note 3.

LIGHTS

❶ CARRY AN OIL- OR BATTERY-POWERED LANTERN.

❷ NEVER ASSUME THAT PROPER LIGHTS WILL BE SHOWN.

❸ BE SURE THE LIGHTS ARE WHAT THEY SHOULD BE BEFORE HASTY ACTION.

1. If the lights aboard go, hoist a lantern, preferably on the backstay. If hoisted to the spreaders, it will not be seen from leeward. See ELECTRICS.

2. Despite the International Rules, incorrect lights are often shown. Fishing boats are prime culprits, but yachts and merchant ships can also be offenders.

3. Always attempt to discern exactly what lights are being shown where on an approaching vessel before taking evasive action. Lifewise, even in approved anchorages, always hoist an anchor light.

4. Strobe lights, *not* in accordance with the International Rules, should be used only for distress and then only when necessary, as they can confuse a watch officer on the bridge of a large ship.

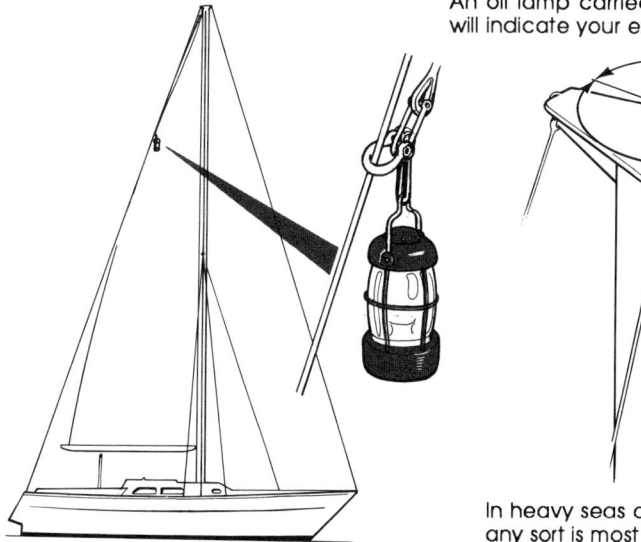

An oil lamp carried in the rigging will indicate your existence.

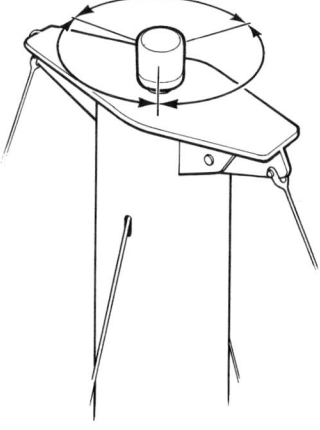

In heavy seas a masthead light of any sort is most likely to be seen.

MAN OVERBOARD

❶ IMMEDIATELY THROW A BUOYANCY DEVICE OVERBOARD, PREFERABLY WITH FLAGGED POLE AND SELF-ACTIVATING LIGHT.

❷ HAVE ONE CREW MEMBER KEEP WATCH ONLY ON THE MAN OVERBOARD, NO MATTER WHAT.

❸ IF UNDER SAIL, TURN UPWIND.

❹ IF UNDER POWER, LOWER THROTTLE.

❺ COMMENCE PICK-UP PROCEDURES.

1. All boats should have a life ring with man-overboard pole, flag, whistle, light and possibly a sea anchor attached. A horseshoe buoy will be easier for the person in the water to slip into. For the pole to be sighted, it must be at least 8 feet (2.5m) long with a bright orange flag attached to the top. In heavy seas even this will be difficult to spot, and a longer pole is not a bad idea. Equally, the flag should be as large as is practical to aid in sighting. A whistle will help in locating the victim in any weather, while a light, preferably self-activating, will be a necessity in low-visibility conditions and at night. Sea anchors are often in bad repute, but a small cloth cone on a long bridle will certainly slow any drift and permit easier spotting and a more planned pick-up. No matter what the equipment, it should be mounted *outboard* of all rails, lifelines and deck encumbrances. Nothing can be worse than to attempt to release the gear and have it foul where it may be impossible to release it. Ideally, devices must be mounted on both sides of the cockpit at the stern within reach and ready-release by the helmsman. The pole can be fitted into a special release socket or very lightly lashed to the backstay. *Very lightly* is important: the lashings must break only through the intertial pull of the life ring or horseshoe. Obviously, the idea is to have the entire kit in the water and as close to the man overboard as quickly as possible. Conditions exist where the shock of falling overboard will be enough to totally disorient and weaken the victim. It becomes absolutely necessary to get the flotation device to him or her and as near as possible quickly. In addition, the victim may have been hurt or possibly incapacitated in the fall. Finally, in heavy going and cold, survival chances are greatly lessened, and the less activity required of the

See note 4.

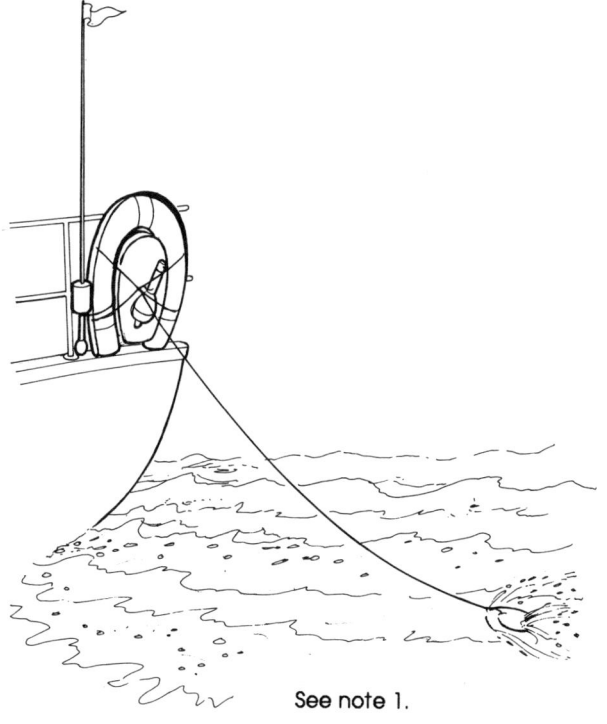

See note 1.

person in the water, the less the heat loss and the chance of hypothermia.

2. As mentioned above, it is not easy to see someone in heavy seas. It is actually difficult to see a man overboard in almost any weather. The need for a crew member with good eyes and better powers of concentration is obvious. But for such a person to be truly effective, he must be left alone, not bothered, not expected to do anything but *keep an eye on the victim!* This cannot be too highly stressed. If the man in the water is lost sight of for even an instant, he may never again be spotted. Certainly, every sailor has practiced man overboard drills, but usually in gentle conditions and without panic or the sense of urgency required when a real living mass of flesh goes over the side. It's a lot different in reality.

3. Once the flotation materials are launched and a spotter is at work, then and only then should maneuvers to recover the person take place. Under sail, turn into the wind. This will allow the boat to keep way, yet slow her down by enough to prepare the crew for recovery measures. What you want to do is to get into a position to be able to pick up the man in the water from windward. (See MAN OVERBOARD: SAVE.)

4. Under power, there is less to do on working the boat, but perhaps greater potential danger to the victim. Under "slow ahead" describe a circle in the water so that you approach the person in the water from behind and to windward. When you are in drifting reach or just alongside (the forward third of the hull), *stop the propellers from turning.* Obviously, you can throw the gears into neutral. In calm weather, shut off the engine if you are in clear water. The danger from the propellers is frightening, and cases are on record of persons being dismembered or killed by a fast-turning prop. On a powerboat, the freeboard, even aft (except on a fishing boat) will be appreciably higher than aboard a similar-length sailing vessel. If a stern door or swim platform is available, the person can best be hauled up from there. However, getting a soaked body up a meter or more of slick topsides is a maneuver that demands some forethought.

Lifeline netting will keep small children as well as deck gear from going overboard.

MAN OVERBOARD: Save

❶ GET TO WINDWARD OF MAN OVERBOARD.

❷ COME ABOUT.

❸ LEAVE FORESAIL BACKED.

❹ LET MAINSHEET FLY.

❺ SECURE HELM TO LEEWARD.

❻ AS BOAT DRIFTS SLOWLY TOWARD PERSON IN WATER, PREPARE TO GET HIM OR HER ON BOARD.

1. What you are doing in the above steps is *heaving to*. It allows the abandonment of actual sailing work, and the best apportionment of crew for retrieving the person in the water. Boat speed can be easily corrected by using the main or repositioning the rudder for angle or drift.

2. Depending on what course you are at the time of the accident, different maneuvers are more or less appropriate for successful positioning of the boat. See the diagrams.

3. If you cannot see the person overboard and conditions are good, sail or motor a reciprocal course. If the weather is foul or shows signs of deteriorating, begin a search upwind of the approximate position you lost your crew. Keep records of time and distance sailed, and take into account current, tides and wind speed, all of which will affect the drift of the person in the water to a much greater degree than the ship. The search may be carried out to windward, on a reach or running. In each case you will have to tack back and forth, running parallel lines over the search area.

4. Once you have him spotted, and the boat is under control, you must be prepared to get him into the boat. An average man in foul weather gear and several layers of clothing will add as much as 50 pounds (23.5 kilos) to his dry weight with immersion. This is not inconsiderable, and must be taken into account in any maneuver to get him back on board. *Note: The man in the water should practice a few precautionary measures to prolong his strength and chances of survival. He must keep his clothing on to preserve body heat. He must not scream or attempt to swim toward the*

boat. *This will only confuse the crew and deplete his energies. He should utilize the gear thrown to him if possible and wait, activating any light and using the whistle only when the mother ship is in sight. Above all, do not panic!*

5. To get the survivor on board, several methods are possible. If he is injured or exhausted, lower a sail with all corners secured by lines to the ship. If he can do some of the work himself, a bosun's chair or bight of rope can be lowered to swing around his arms, allowing him to sit in it and be winched aboard. If a platform or boarding ladder is permanently attached to the stern, have him grab a bight of rope and manuever him to the stern with a crew member on each quarter to assist boarding. In boats with transom-mounted rudders, a set of steps can be installed on the rudder blade from below the water line to allow easier boarding. *Do not attempt to haul the victim aboard by his arms!*

6. Singlehanded sailors have the most to worry about in man-overboard situations. You must always trail a poly (floating) line with a buoy attached to the end of it. This should be about 25 meters long. If you are sailing under self-steering gear, some means of disengaging the gear is necessary. One possibility is suggested in the illustration. A permanently mounted ladder with a lanyard attached to release the lower half, or the transom steps mentioned above, should be included in fitting out the boat. In powerboats, the trailing line must be bridled to avoid fouling the propeller and might be rigged either to shift the gears into neutral or shut down the ignition when given a sharp jerk.

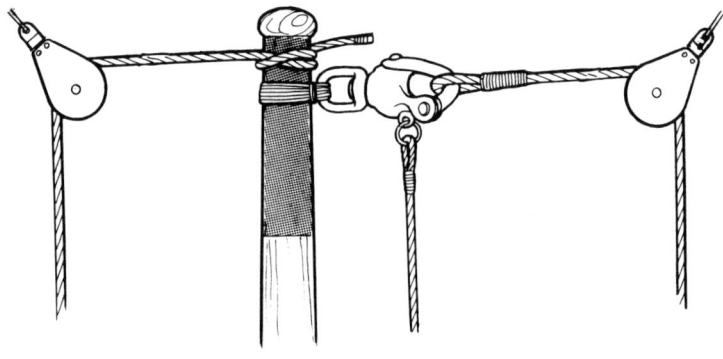

See note 6.

See note 3.

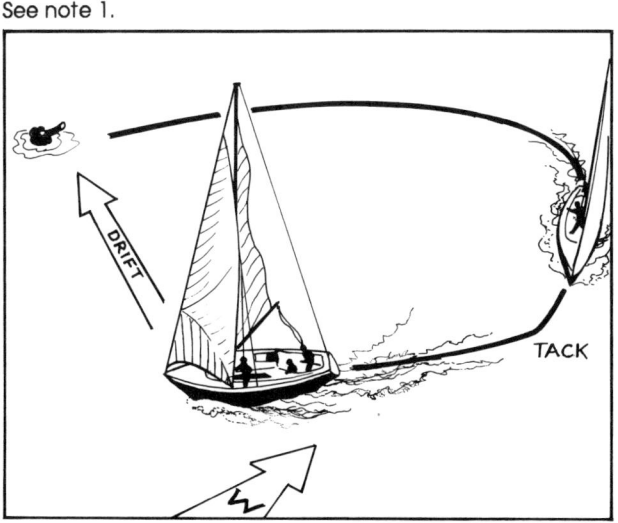

TIME 1735
DISTANCE SAILED 3/4 M
CURRENT WESTERLY
WIND SPEED 15 knts
DIRECTION SSE
TIDE 35 m to high

See notes 4 & 5.

See note 1.

DRIFT

TACK

MAST CLIMBING

❶ A HALYARD HAS FOULED, A TANG FRACTURED, ETC.

❷ REDUCE THE BOAT SPEED AND HEAD OFF ON A REACH.

❸ RIG BOSUN'S CHAIR ON SPARE HALYARD.

❹ HAVE CREW MEMBER STATIONED AT WINCH.

❺ RIG DOWNHAUL AND SAFETY LINE.

❻ CRANK UP.

1. First ascertain if there is a way to free the line or ignore the damage without going up. If you are near port, you may be able to jury-rig an arrangement to get you in without trying to work in a seaway at the masthead. Remember, the pitching moment is much greater high up, especially if 75 kilos of mass is suddenly hanging on for dear life. Most repair jobs at the top are two-handed affairs, and for effective work both body and legs must be secured and braced. If any possible way exists to carry on without clambering up, take it, *unless the crew or ship will be endangered through failure to take action.*

2. Tearing along at hull speed will in no way aid the crew who must be at the masthead, either once there or climbing. Lower the boat speed as much as possible while maintaining steering way. A reach will steady the boat and, depending upon the tack, can actually provide a more secure position at mast top. Sail may have to be reduced.

3. The traditional bosun's chair is both uncomfortable and potentially dangerous. The wood seat can slam into the mast, causing more damage. The newer, all-cloth models with restraining straps and tool pockets can be both safer and allow for more efficient and quicker work. The crew who has volunteered to go up must be *totally* secured before ascending. A downhaul must be rigged to the chair, and a line with snap hook or some other expedient means of wrapping around the mast to keep the occupant in position should be affixed, preferably around the person, not just to the seat. A safety harness can be employed, providing that the tether is not too long. All the tools that might be needed should be secured by lanyards if possible. In fact, it is a good idea to keep basic tools

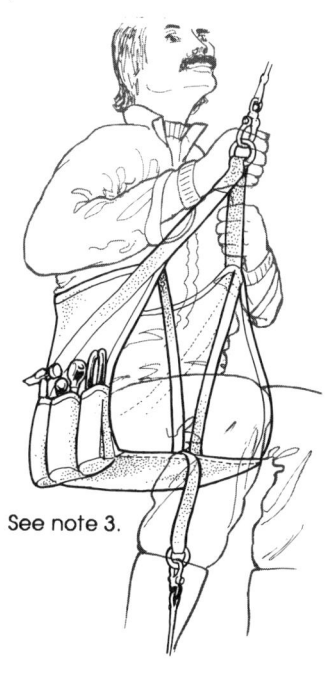

See note 3.

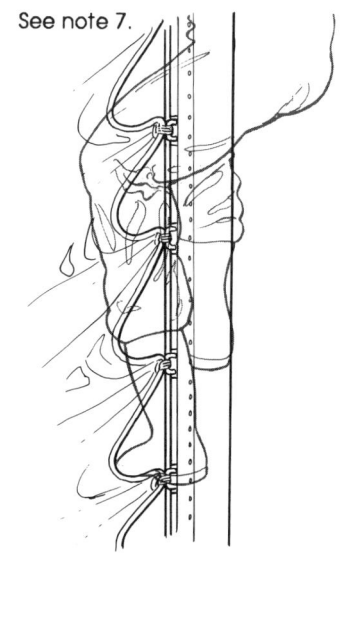

See note 7.

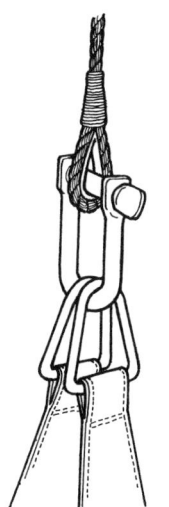

Make sure halyard shackles are positive-lock type and secure.

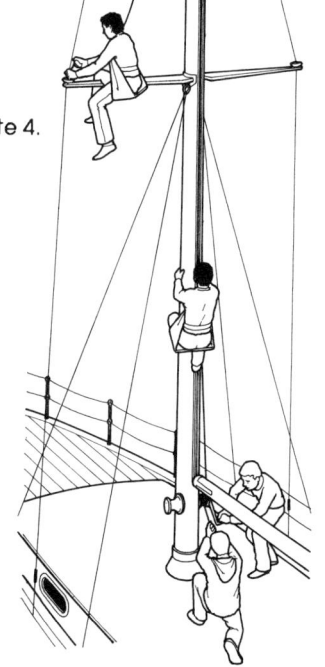

See note 4.

permanently ensconced with the bosun's chair: visegrips, screwdriver, marlinspike, adjustable wrench/spanner, etc. The assumption of rigging the chair on a spare halyard demands some forethought. Spinnaker halyards may be too light to be safe, the main halyard may be jammed, and the jib needed to maintain forward motion. In such a situation, it may be wise to use the spinnaker halyard as a messenger to carry a heavier line through its masthead sheave. In a fractionally rigged boat, a spare main halyard might well be permanently rigged.

4. Hauling a person aloft demands a strong wincher, enough turns (at least four) around the winch and a good braking turn around a cleat. The point is to get someone up safely, not fast. A second crew member on the deck should handle the downhaul, keeping it taut and making sure that swing is kept to a minimum. If the main is down, the safety line should be used by the man aloft, breaking it only at the spreaders.

5. Frankly, the precautions mentioned above should be adhered to in *all* weathers. At night, a flashlight/torch should be carried aloft, possibly taped to the upper arm with gaffer's tape. Gloves are another recommendation, but they must be full-fingered and leather. Anything else will either chafe or slip. Deck boots will protect the legs and a foam-filled life vest will help absorb bumps while not overly hindering the wearer's movements.

6. If for some reason the bosun's chair is not usable or one isn't on board, a substitute will have to be devised. Lots of possibilities exist, of course, but whatever is used must be of irreproachable integrity: a bowline on a bight or an emergency boarding ladder. Do *not* use a fender unless it is the type that allows the line to run through it; standard inflatable fenders are not reliable enough in their grommeting to hold a man's weight under stress conditions. And, should you use one of the other alternatives, remember to pad it well. Raw wood or rope can cause serious injury aloft in high winds and rolling conditions. The poor sucker at the masthead has enough to worry about!

7. There will be times when no halyard is available for hauling a bosun's chair. A rope or plastic ladder, or a wood and rope ladder, can be used but demands much vigilance and agility as well as a messenger line to haul it up: it's usually far too much bother and too time-consuming when you need it. The main can be slacked slightly (only in fairly large boats) and used as a ladder. However, the slides *must* be metal. Plastic slugs can fracture, causing a rapid descent of catastrophic speed and force. Follow safety precautions!

MEDICAL EMERGENCY

❶ DO YOU NEED TO SAVE A LIFE?

❷ DO YOU NEED TO PREVENT THE SITUATION FROM GETTING WORSE?

❸ MUST YOU RELIEVE PAIN AND SUFFERING?

❹ DO YOU NEED OUTSIDE ASSISTANCE?

1. The above questions are not meant to solve any specific problem, but they must be asked in any situation concerning injury or sickness. Though most accidents aboard will be minor—cuts, seasickness, sunburn, colds and flu—many others will require more than two aspirin and a cup of tea. You must be prepared to cope with anything short of major surgery, especially if you intend a transoceanic passage of any length. To this degree, *every* yacht should be equipped with an up-to-date and constantly renewed first-aid kit, including appropriate medications for the areas to which you plan to voyage. Also aboard must be a modern first-aid manual *that has been read by at least two crew.* Any member of the crew who has a specific chronic ailment, drug allergy or medication requirement should inform the captain of such *before* setting sail. It is up to the captain to assess the situation and make the decision of the crew's suitability based on the remoteness of the landfall, the conditions likely to be encountered and the general physical condition of the crew member.

2. If the person has stopped breathing or has no discernable heartbeat you must act immediately to save that person's life. Bleeding will kill a person much less quickly, unless it is a major hemorrhage of an artery, than lack of oxygen or no heartbeat.

3. If the person is not subject to any immediate threat, you must decide if the condition might worsen. Many injuries and illnesses can get more serious, but the most common might include: burns, infections, exposure, poisoning, concussion, fractures, unconsciousness, open wounds and chest pain. If you decide that the person is in no immediate danger, continue to port. Otherwise, consult your medical guide.

4. The greatest concurrent problem with any injury at sea may be fear. Not only take appropriate action, but reassure the injured

person. Care, concern and will can play as important a part as anything to help alleviate distress and aid someone on the path to recovery.

5. Can you cope? Certain medical conditions will be beyond your ability to treat. If you are far from shore, you must use your judgment and common sense, and do everything in your power to aid the patient with what you have at hand. Certain infections can be held at bay with antibiotics. Certain fractures can be immobilized until a doctor is at hand. But other conditions may be impossible to do much about. Internal hemorrhaging, heart attack, certain types of poisoning, extreme hypothermia may be beyond you.

TREATMENT AND DIAGNOSIS

Following are some general guidelines for treatment and diagnosis. They should be used in conjuction with a reliable medical first-aid manual. They are not infallible, and any responsibility is in the hands of the person administering the first aid.

Abdominal pain: This can be mild or severe. Until the cause is clear:
>Put the patient to rest.
>Allow neither food nor liquids.
>Do not give laxatives.
>Give pain medication if required.

If pain is persistent, vomiting frequent, diarrhea severe, abdomen firm and tender, seek medical assistance. Very severe pain accompanied by very hard, tender abdomen can indicate ruptured appendix, ulcer or ovarian cyst. Infection is possible and antibiotics every six hours should be considered until professional advice is secured.

Antibiotics do *not* cure everything! They are useless against viral or fungal infections. Follow doctor's recommendations closely as to dosage and types to carry aboard. Duration of treatment should be no more than a week to ten days. Cautions:
>Avoid sunlight.
>Never give to pregnant women or children under eight without specific medical advice.
>Allergic reactions or lack of response should indicate need for immediate medical consultation.

Bleeding: Use sterile, soft, absorbent material and apply pressure. Small cuts will usually stop bleeding after a short while; larger cuts should have the material taped over until further action can be

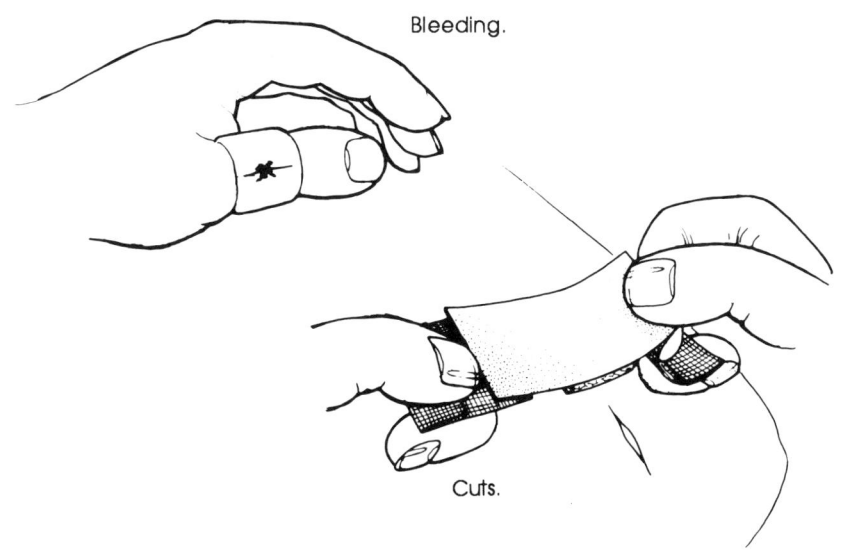

Bleeding.

Cuts.

taken. Cleanse with soap and water or hydrogen peroxide. Use a tourniquet only in extreme, heavy bleeding emergencies.

Burns: For all burns, the immediate treatment is to apply cold water liberally. Used soaked cloths, either fresh or salt water. Avoid running water and ointments, creams or sprays. With anything more than a first-degree burn, cover with sterile petroleum jelly, gauze and a sterile dressing. For second-and-third degree burns seek immediate medical attention. Life-threatening burns can cause shock and the danger of infection. Give oral fluids, keep dressings in place, give pain killes and antibiotics if more than twenty-four hours will elapse before a doctor can care for the patient.

Cardiopulmonary arrest: Heart attack or lung malfunction. Follow these steps:
    Determine consciousness.
    Open the airway, tilt back the head with neck lifted.
    Give mouth-to-mouth resuscitation; if after four breaths the
        chest doesn't move, attempt Heimlich maneuver.
    Feel for pulse. If there, but no breathing, start mouth-to-mouth
        at one breath per five seconds.
    If no pulse, start CPR (see below).

CPR: Your local Red Cross offers training in this lifesaving technique. If you haven't taken the course, follow the steps below only if the situation is genuinely desperate:

Place victim on hard surface.

Place the heel of the hand over the sternum about 2 inches from the lower tip.

Place the other hand at right angles on top of the first and press down hard enough to depress the breastplate an inch or two. Release. Pause. Repeat.

Give victim two breaths after each ten to fifteen depressions.

This is about the correct rate.

Choking: Use the Heimlich manuever.

Deliver back thumps with a closed fist between the shoulder blades.

With hands clasped around the victim, make abdominal thrusts between the breastplate and the navel: four thumps, four thrusts.

Continue until choking is relieved.

Cold: Wear loose-fitting warm clothes; keep hands, feet and head covered. Get out of wet clothes as soon as possible. Drink and eat warm substances. Do *not* drink alcohol.

Constipation: Eat lots of fruits, vegetables and roughage. Colace is usually effective and convenient to take. Avoid laxatives. A glycerine suppository or a warm-water enema may be best with prolonged constipation.

Cuts: Use strip or butterfly bandages to close the cut, apply pressure and keep it clean. Larger cuts will require stitching and prompt medical attention. If signs of infection appear, use antibiotics.

Diarrhea: Keep up fluid intake; most patent medicines will make the patient feel better but will *not* cure the cause. Pepto-Bismol may be the best, according to a recent study. If the diarrhea is accompanied by high fever or bloody stools, use ampicillin as per directions. Seek medical care as soon as possible.

Eyes: For eye irritations, glare, foreign bodies, wash with fresh water, cover with loose-fitting bandages. Seek medical care if pain or visual impairment persists. Always wear sunglasses.

Fever: Use aspirin or acetaminophen, no more than 10 grains every four hours. Do *not* increase dosage. Cool sponge baths can aid in reducing fever. Dress the person lightly unless suffering chills. If fever is high and persists, infection is possible and antibiotics are called for. If no change after forty-eight hours, seek immediate medical attention.

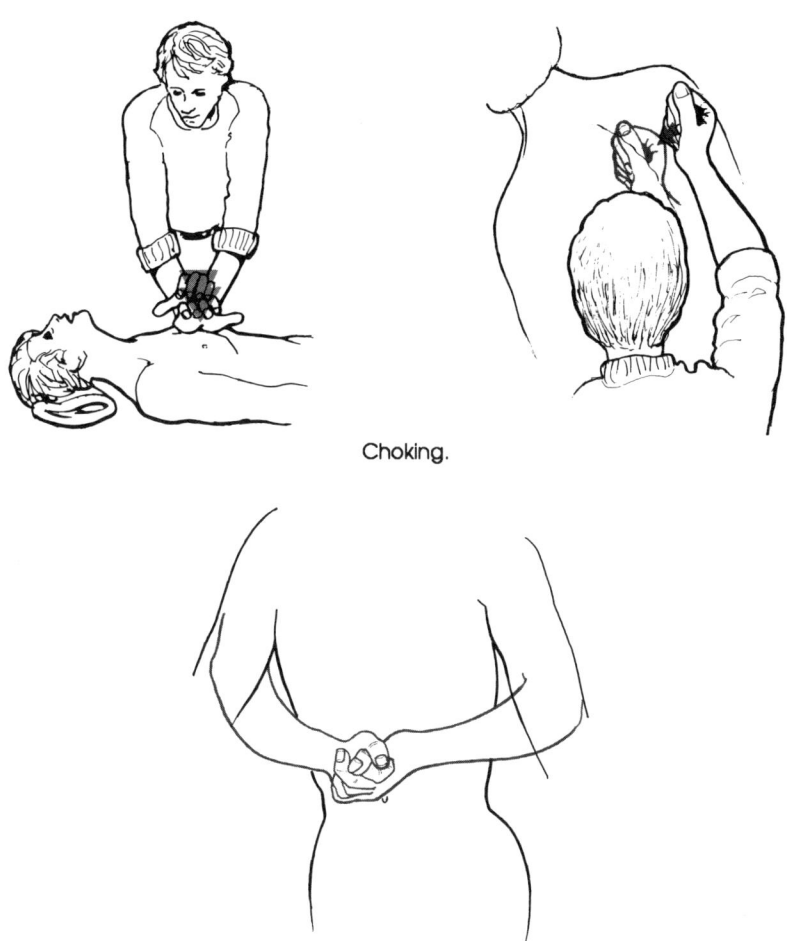

Choking.

Fractures: Immobilize immediately. Apply ice packs if possible. Give pain medication. Do *not* try to set the fracture, merely keep it from moving with splints or bandages. Keep tight enough but not so tight as to stop or hinder circulation. Seek medical aid immediately. Compound fractures, where skin has been broken, will require cleansing of the wound and antibiotics.

Frostbite: Warm affected part rapidly in 40 to 42 degree C. water. Pain medication may be needed. Seek medical assistance. If unavailable, apply warm soaks twice a day, clean dressings and separation of toes and fingers will prevent tissue deterioration.

Heat: Keep protected, even on cool days. Drink what you need to feel comfortable. Do *not* ration water. The body can store water and the old saw about rationing has been fairly convincingly disproved by recent U.S. Army Survival School studies. If heatstroke occurs, intensive, rapid cooling is called for. Put victim in cold-water bath (plugged cockpit) or wrap in soaked sheets. Sea water works well. After body temperature has dropped to 102° (40.6° C), cease cold treatment. Massage arms and legs to promote cooling circulation. As soon as possible start feeding cool liquids by mouth. Follow-up medical care is necessary as potentially serious damage can be inflicted on internal organs.

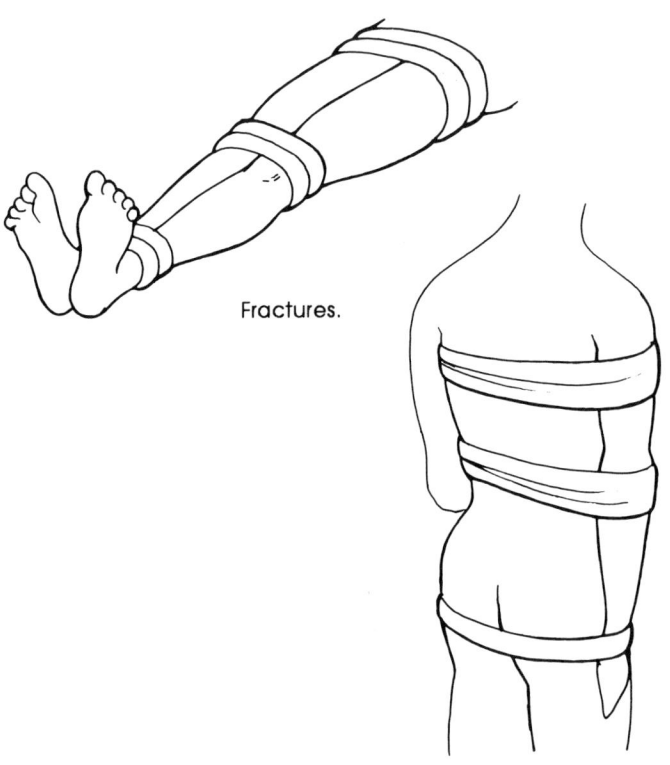

Fractures.

Pain: Pain is a symptom. Specific medication will not cure the cause unless the cause is known. For relief: aspirin, acetaminophen. For medium pain, codeine, Darvon, Percodan, Talwin; these all require prescriptions. Ask your doctor for specifics. Severe and persistent pain: morphine or Demerol. These are dangerous drugs and should be avoided for all but the transoceanic passagemaker. Ask for specifics from your doctor.

Poisoning: Internal—cause vomiting as soon as possible, except for petroleum products; after vomiting stops give milk, mineral oil, or bread to absorb the poison and keep it from absorption into the system. Skin contact—wash thoroughly with water, remove clothing. Breathing—get into fresh air immediately. So many poisons exist it is well to contact a doctor by radio as soon as you are able to. He may be able to help. If the victim is comatose, get to land immediately, even if it means calling for air rescue.

Respiratory infections: The infection cures itself. Flu, colds, sore throat, bronchitis are best treated with rest, lots of fluids, aspirin, decongestants, etc. In cases where fever develops or persists and no improvement is seen, antibiotics may be called for. They should be taken for ten days, even after symptoms have disappeared.

Seasickness: The most effective medication I know is Bucladin. This is a prescription drug better known in the U.K. than in the U.S. Some changes have occurred in the composition over the years. According to *The Yachtsman's Guide to First Aid Afloat*, by Earl Rubell, M.D., the correct formula should be:

Buclizine HC1	50/0mg
Pyridoxine HC1	10/0mg
Scopolamine HBr	0/2mg
Atropine SO4	0/05mg
Hyoscamine SO4	0/05mg

Patent medicines work or don't work according to the individual. Chronic seasickness must be dealt with as best one can. Milder forms can often be cured by focusing on a distant horizon, keeping blood sugar levels up, and avoiding interiors or exaggerated sense of motion.

Shock: You can help prevent shock by keeping the victim warm, dry, reassured and breathing regularly. If the victim goes into shock, there is little that can be done without transfusion and medical facilities.

Urinary infections: Nonspecific—drink lots of fluids; Pyridium can be administered to relieve burning and frequency of urination. Wait a week before administering anything else. If infection persists, administer Gantrisin or tetracycline. Seek medical advice. Specific (venereal)—gonorrhea symptoms (discharge, burning urination) are treated with antibiotics and medical follow-up. Syphilis can be diagnosed as a painless ulcer at the point of sexual contact. Seek medical advice immediately. Syphilis is a complicated disease and is beyond the scope of any first-aid treatment.

PROPELLER

❶ IF PROP FOULS, TURN OFF ENGINE IMMEDIATELY.

❷ IF NEAR SHORE, ANCHOR.

❸ IF OFFSHORE, HEAVE TO.

❹ SEE DIVING.

❺ CUT IMPEDIMENT FREE.

1. Failure to shut down engine could cause damage to the gearbox.

2. Since a crewmember will have to dive to clear the obstruction, follow the methods set out in the section on DIVING. Stopping the vessel will aid immeasurably. Try to anchor out of a tidal stream and be sure that anyone going overboard is tethered to ship.

3. It may help to raise the stern of the boat by concentrating weights forward. Also, a partially inflated dinghy can make a useful work area as well as cushioning the stern in any sort of swell. In heavy seas and well away from land, towing warps or a drogue may keep the boat at a reasonable speed and allow steerage. Do not attempt to go overboard in these conditions. Danger from the pitching, heaving hull is too great.

4. It will probably be easier to saw rather than cut the rope turns on the prop. A hacksaw blade or keyhole saw will be most effective and can be lashed to a makeshift wood handle.

See note 4.

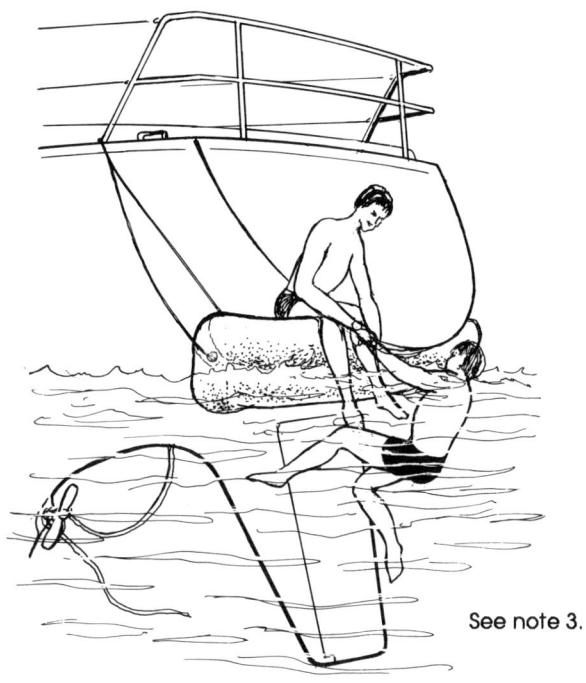

See note 3.

PUMPS: Bilge

❶ IF BILGE PUMP CLOGS, DISASSEMBLE AT ONCE, REMOVE DE-BRIS.

❷ IF PUMP STILL WILL NOT FUNCTION, CHECK THE DIAPHRAGM, REPLACE IF NECESSARY.

❸ IF DRAW IS MINIMAL, CHECK STRUM BOXES (STRAINERS) AT TERMINATION OF HOSES.

❹ IF HANDLE BREAKS, USE SHORT SECTION OF PIPE, CUT TO FIT FEMALE PUMP HANDLE RECEPTACLE.

❺ NAVY-TYPE PUMPS MAY NEED TOTAL DISASSEMBLY.

1. Most modern bilge pumps are of the diaphragm type. These will function in situations where older pumps would have long since failed or clogged. However, even a pump that has a capacity of 30 gallons per minute (115 liters) will not be very effective with a major hull breach. In such a case, only an engine-driven pump will suffice. And if the engine ceases to function, a bucket brigade will do far more than either.

2. Always carry spares for all pumps. A new diaphragm can be installed in approximately five minutes, providing access is reasonable. The same is true of strainers; you must be able to reach them.

3. Installation is vital to proper pump efficiency and safety. Too often, bilge pumps are mounted so that a cockpit locker lid must be opened to operate them. Mount cockpit pump with a through-deck fitting, properly capped and watertight and accessible to the helmsman. Any offshore boat should have a second pump operable from below. Most stock boats are equipped with pumps of much too small capacity. Minimum should be 25 gallons per minute (95 liters).

4. Pump handles will break. Either keep a factory spare, make sure the interior and exterior pumps have identical handles or carry a hardwood dowel or length of pipe of correct dimensions. Also, it is a good idea to drill a hole through the handle and tie it with a light lanyard to a spot where it is always at hand, near the pump. A spring clip will also work well.

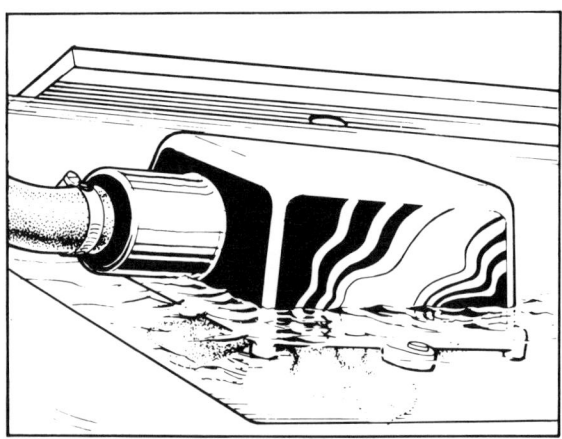

Strum boxes (filters) should be fitted to intake ends of all hoses.

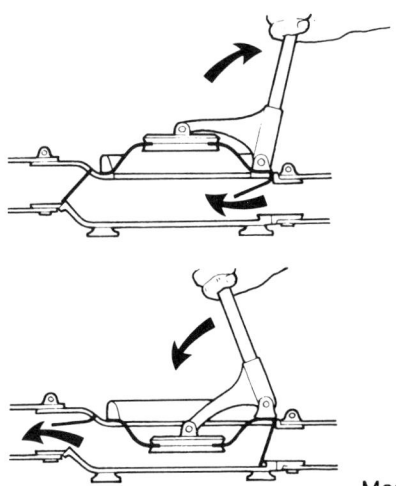

Most pumps are fitted with nonreturn flap valves. Diaphragm forces flaps open and closed.

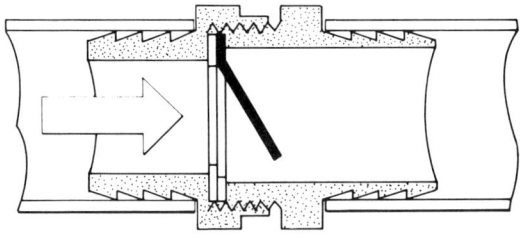

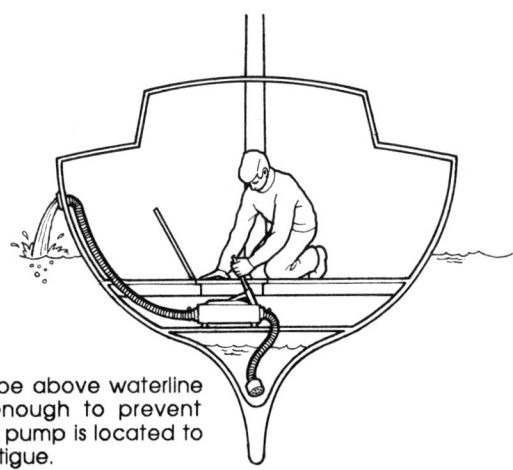

Discharge line must be above waterline and looped high enough to prevent backflow. Make sure pump is located to work with minimum fatigue.

RIGGING

❶ IF ANY PART OF THE STANDING RIGGING FAILS, *IMMEDIATELY* REMOVE OR DECREASE STRAIN ON THAT SIDE OF THE RIG.

❷ TACK, DO NOT JIBE.

❸ JURY-RIG A REPLACEMENT OR REPAIR.

1. Depending on conditions, you can continue sailing. However, if calm, and forestay fails, it's best to let well enough alone, rather than risk the chance of the mast falling aft into the cockpit. When things start getting rough, such luxuries will not be possible and getting the sails down and the rigging break mended will be most important. If the backstay breaks, lead a halyard aft and tension with a Spanish windlass or block and tackle–the vang, perhaps. You will head up during this process. If the forestay ruptures, head downwind, then use a spare halyard shackled to the stemhead for support. If the halyard is long enough, this can be led aft to a winch for greater tensioning.

2. Should a shroud go, immediately tack–jibing will place undue strain on the rig, and could carry it away–and head off so as to put the least strain on the failed part of the rig. Try to take sea state into account, as undue pitching and rolling can cause almost as much damage as the original fitting letting go.

3. Your most useful equipment for jury-rigging, besides a spare halyard, will be wire rope or bulldog clips. These should be galvanized, not stainless steel, which has a tendency to slip. If a stay has fractured at the turnbuckle fitting end, form a bight or loop with the wire and use at least two clips to form an eye, which may be lashed or shackled to the turnbuckle or attached directly to the chainplate with a block and tackle. If the stay has broken at the masthead, sooner or later someone will have to go aloft. If no spare length of wire is aboard, the eye should be made at the end of wire aloft (do this while still on deck), which can then be shackled to the masthead fitting or tang. The now shorter stay can be attached to the chainplate or turnbuckle with shackles and a length of chain. If the wire has broken midway, make two eyes and fasten them with shackles, lashings or chain.

4. Rarely does it occur, but when a turnbuckle fractures or lets go, the solution is actually much simpler than when the shroud or stay

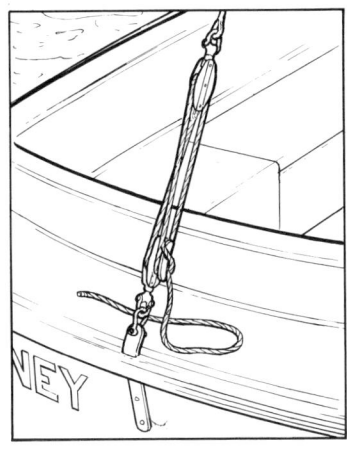

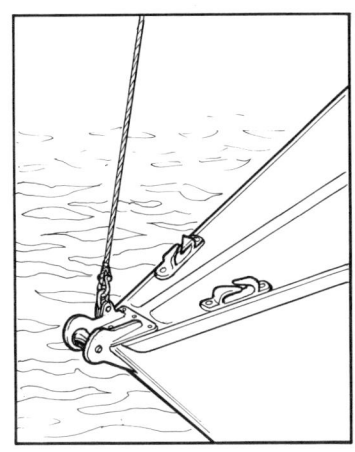

See note 1.

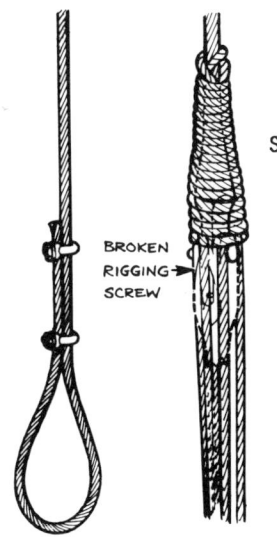

See note 3.

BROKEN
RIGGING →
SCREW

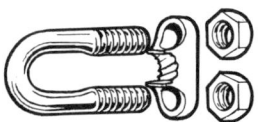

See note 5.

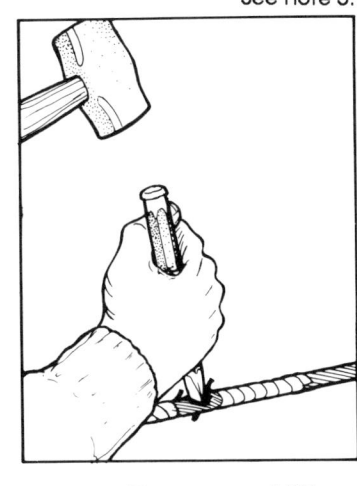

breaks. Either replace it with another turnbuckle, use a lanyard or lash the stay in place. Times come, though, when the turnbuckle is frozen tight. This is the result of lax maintenance, and you should curse yourself soundly. Since you are presumably sailing on a tack that takes the strain off the fitting, remove the offender by slipping a clevis, lash the stay temporarily, and use two mole wrenches to break the freeze. Replace the turnbuckle.

5. Should wire need to be cut, use either wire cutters or a cold chisel. However, whip or tape the wire to either side of the proposed cut first to prevent unlaid strands or eye-damaging bits of flying steel. Wire rope is prone to a life of its own, and another crew member should hold it fast. Lacking the personnel, lash the wire with light stuff to keep it in place.

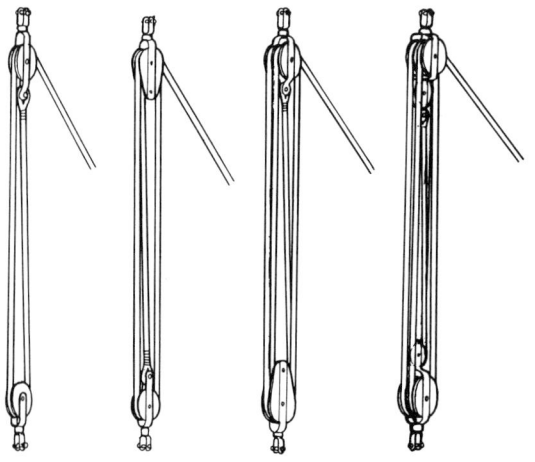

Tackles can be the best tensioning device should a turnbuckle give way. The greater the number of parts, the greater the force exerted for the effort.

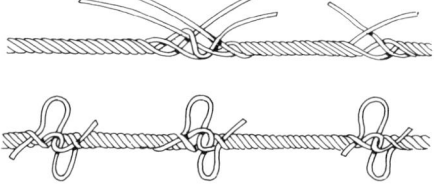

Wire-to-wire and wire-to-rope splices are best performed ashore or at anchor.

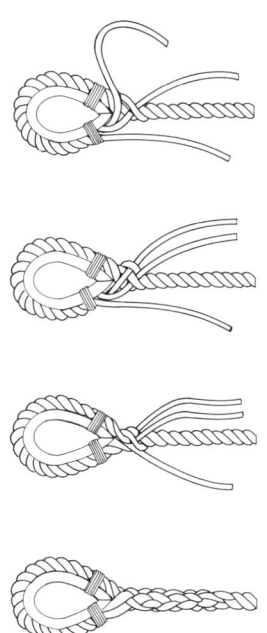

Eye splice with thimble.

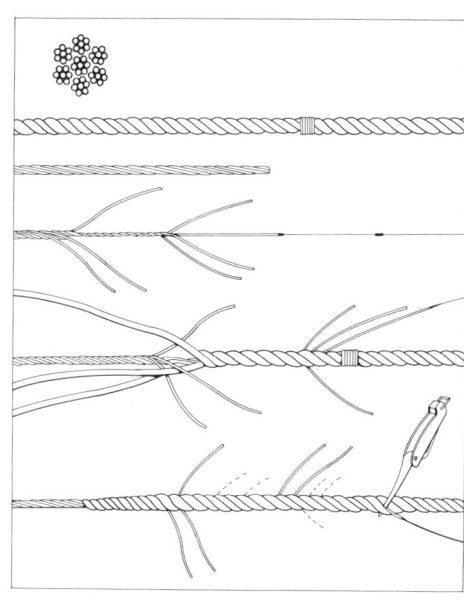

Working wire-to-wire splices can be dangerous. Make sure ends are secured and taped as you go.

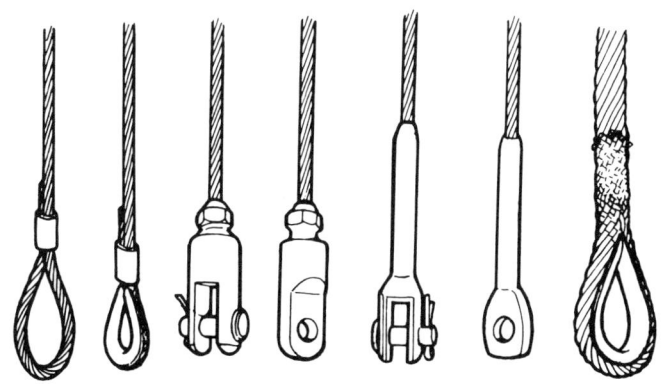

Different end fittings for wire rope. Nicopress/Talurit (1st & 2nd from left) or Sta-Lock/Norseman (3rd & 4th from left) are most practical for on-board repairs.

Timber hitch.

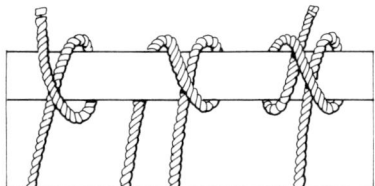

Marline hitch.

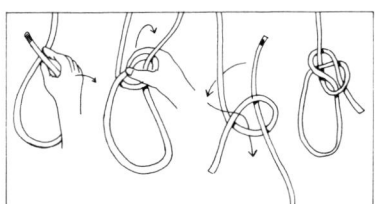

Bowline.

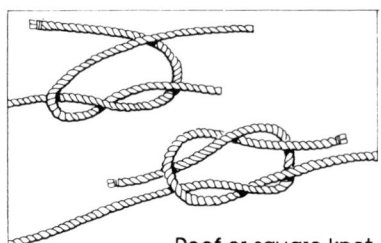

Reef or square knot.

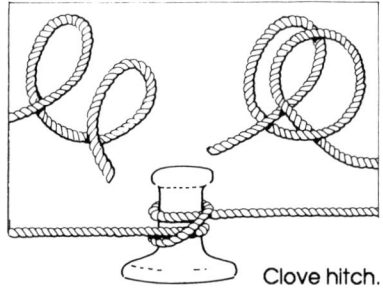

Clove hitch.

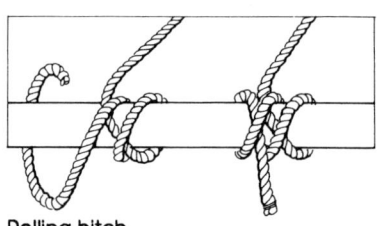

Rolling hitch.

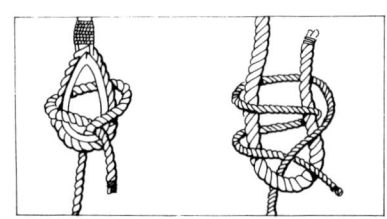

Sheet bend & double sheet bend.

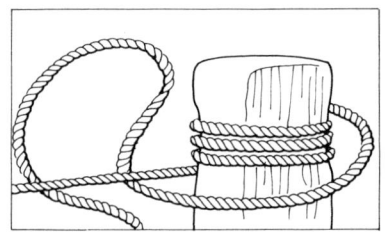

Towing hitch.

SAIL REPAIR

❶ IF MAINSAIL TEARS ALONG A SEAM, REEF.

❷ IF TEAR IS IN CLOTH, PATCH WITH TAPE ON BOTH SIDES.

❸ IF SLIDES RIP OFF, LASH.

❹ IF BOLTROPE TEARS, PATCH.

❺ IF CLEW FITTING FRACTURES, LASH.

1. Should the main rip along a seam, or should the stitching come undone, and the tear is below the reef points, reefing is the simplest immediate solution. If the tear is high up, lower the sail immediately, and continue to sail under foresail alone. Or hoist the storm trysail in its place until repairs can be effected. With roller reefing, there is greater latitude in just how large or small the reef can be, but after a certain point the main will lose any efficiency, driving power or ability to balance the foresail, and should be dropped and replaced.

2. Should the sailcloth, not a seam, tear, best patch it on *both* sides, either with rigging tape or even better, the special self-sticking sail-repair patches sold for the purpose. In calm conditions, patches of sailcloth and "instant" waterproof glue can effect a temporary repair. The best solution is to drop the sail, replace it with another and have the sail sent below for proper stitched repair. A stitched sail repair requires, in synthetic cloths, fine needles, not the canvas-piercing monsters of old, Terylene/Dacron thread, and a comfortable sewing palm. Beeswax is not really necessary with modern materials. Double the thread, knot the two loose ends, and close the tears with a series of herringbone stitches. With synthetic cloth, anything from six to ten stitches per inch, depending on the weight of cloth, thread, etc., should be adequate. If the tear is larger than your four fingers minus the thumb can enter, it should be patched. A patch can be done in several ways. Use approximately the same weight cloth as that of the sail. Use two layers—one on either side—of lighter cloth. Seal or fold under the edges. Tape the patch in place. Fasten using a seam stitch. *Note*: try to line up the weave of the sailcloth and the patch if possible. With very large rips this may not be achievable with the materials at hand. Any patch is better than none. Adhesive-backed sail-repair patches are sold for small jobs. These will usually work

for a while, but are neither permanent nor particularly suited for heavy weather. They can be temporarily used until you or your sailmaker makes a permanent repair.

3. Lost slides are all too common, especially with plastic and nylon. A few spares ought be carried, and can easily be sewn on or, if the sail has been grommeted along its luff, can be lashed with light synthetic twine or tape.

4. Boltropes are easily repaired with a patch around the rope on either side, extending several inches outward from the rope. Sew through on both sides, remembering to keep the patch around the rope as tight as possible, increasing the diameter as little as possible and thus avoiding jams.

5. If the clew fitting goes by the board, a stout lashing will temporarily suffice. More permanently, sew in a new grommet, sew in a rope grommet, sew in a D-ring or O-ring replacement. In any case, make sure that the corner of the sail is heavily reinforced, and the stitching is doubled or quadrupled. All sewn repairs are similar: if overlap is possible, do it. If you can double-stitch, do it. If both sides can be patched, do it.

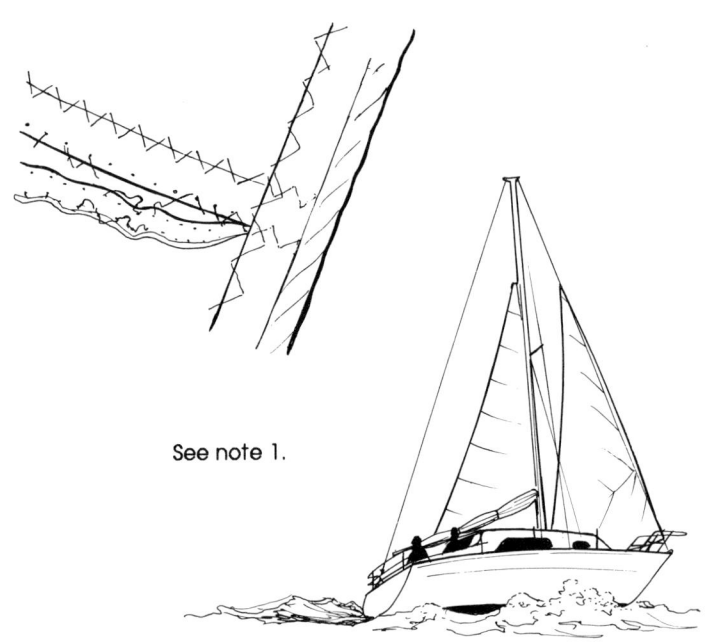

See note 1.

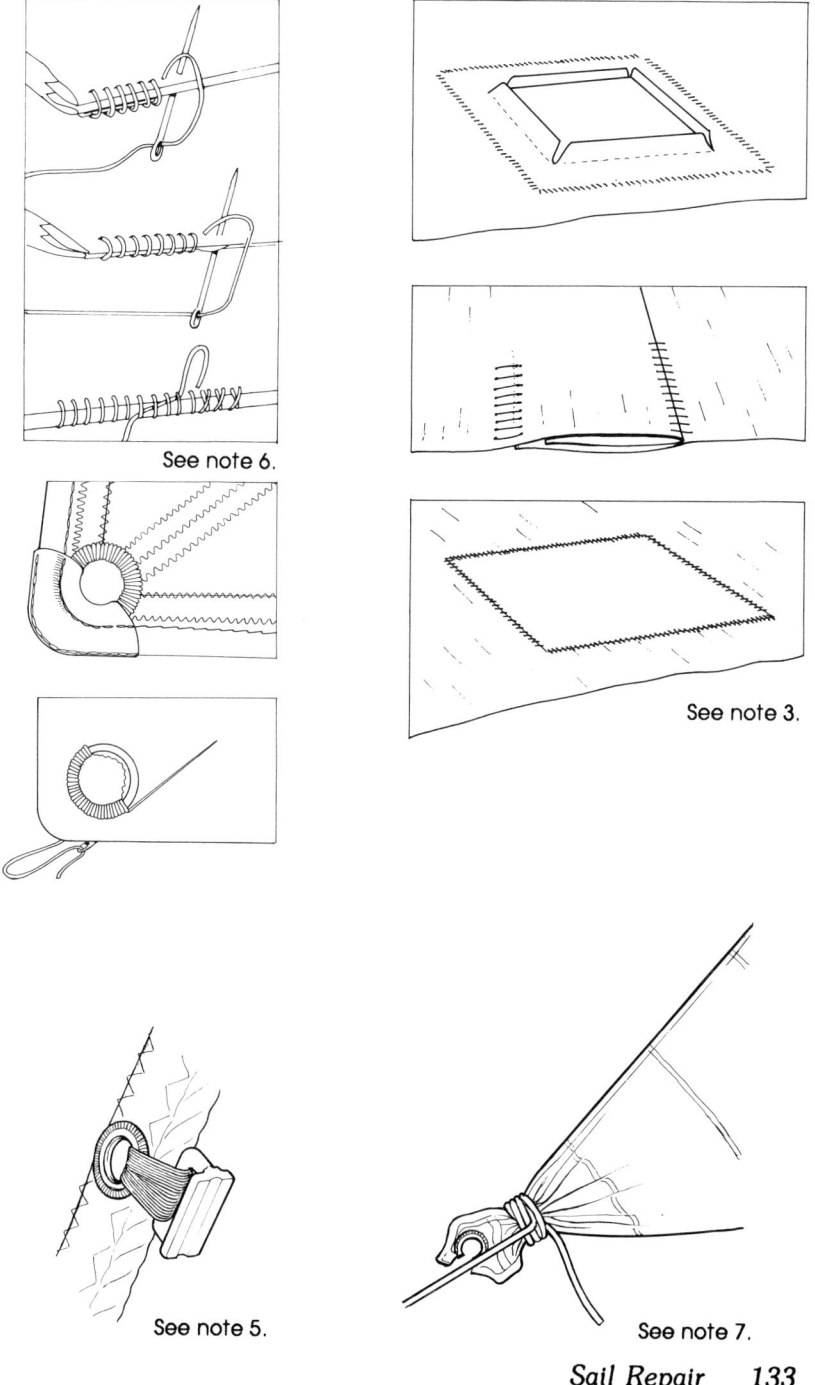

See note 6.

See note 3.

See note 5.

See note 7.

Sail Repair   133

SALVAGE

❶ SALVAGE IS A SUBJECT FRAUGHT WITH DISPUTE AND COMPLICATION.

❷ MAKE A CONTRACT BEFOREHAND IF POSSIBLE.

❸ BE PREPARED TO HANDLE LATER COURT ACTION OR ARBITRATION.

1. A salvor must establish certain proofs to make a claim:
The vessel was in peril.
He made a voluntary decision to aid the distressed vessel.
He risked his life and vessel to save the distressed vessel.
He achieved his aim and succeeded in aiding.

2. If a contract is agreed upon *before* rescue efforts commence, no further claims can be made. A verbal agreement with witnesses present is adequate, legal and binding.

3. No matter what, few claims are settled without court or arbitrator attentions. Be prepared for a long and complicated procedure. Seek legal advice, specialized if necessary. The procedures are not related to land law and can easily overwhelm an amateur.

4. Accepting tows or aid does *not* entitle the aiding party to claim salvage, nor claim ownership of property. Consult a qualified attorney or solicitor to determine the extent of claims or damages.

SIGNALS

❶ BEFORE SENDING OUT ANY SIGNALS MAKE SURE YOU REALLY ARE IN DISTRESS.

❷ USE THE APPROPRIATE SIGNAL.

❸ USE THE SIGNAL ONLY IF THERE IS A FAIR CHANCE IT WILL BE SEEN OR HEARD.

❹ WHEN USING PYROTECHNICS, BE CAUTIOUS.

1. Far too often distress signals are sent for inappropriate reasons or for no reason at all. If the engine has died and you are merely becalmed, *no* reason exists to send any signal. Patience is the solution.

2. Don't use flares in the daytime and smoke signals at night. Don't use an EPIRB when five miles from port. Don't attempt using VHF distress channel in mid-ocean. Common sense should dictate the signal most appropriate for any situation.

3. Equally a question of propriety, don't waste signals, especially pyrotechnics. Unless you are near land, or sight another ship, chances are your visual signal will not be seen. This is especially true of open water passages, a great many of which are away from shipping lanes.

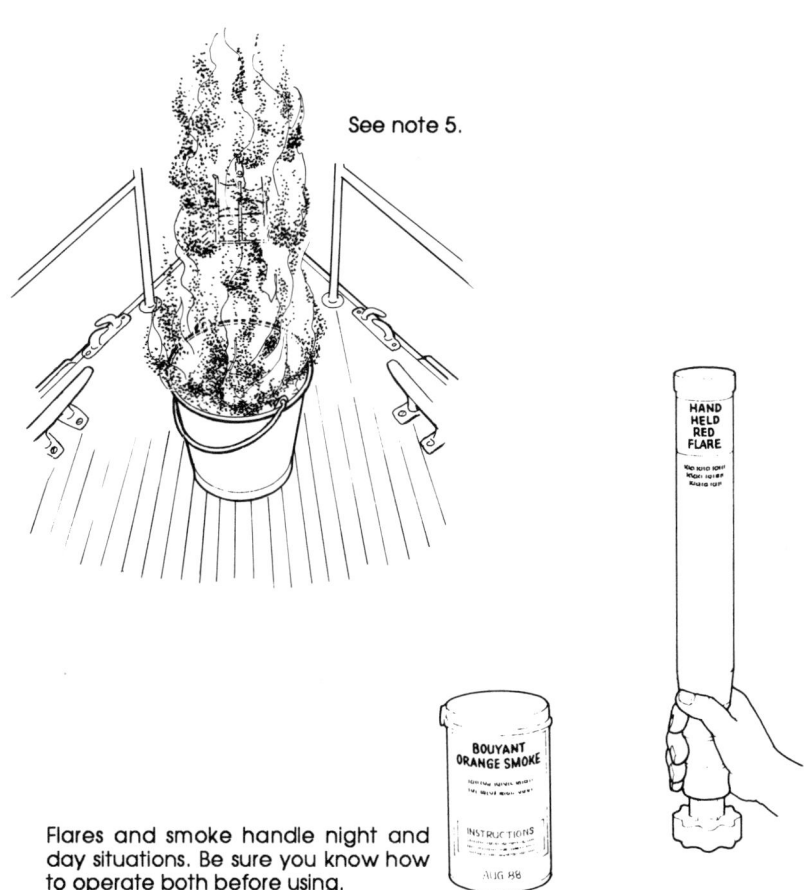

See note 5.

Flares and smoke handle night and day situations. Be sure you know how to operate both before using.

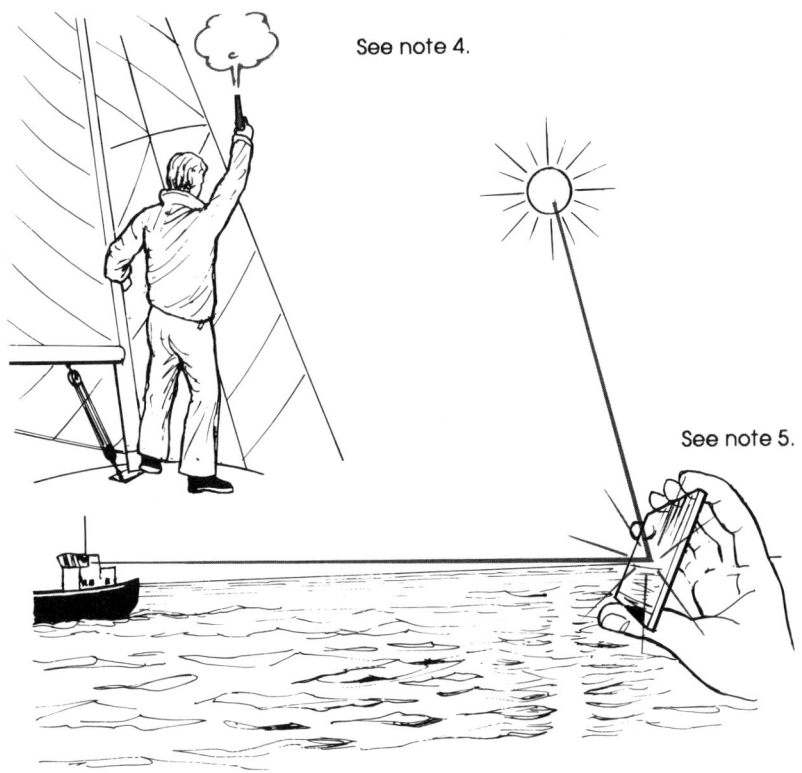

See note 4.

See note 5.

4. Pyrotechnics, either hand-held or fired, must be used with caution. If any way exists to practice legally, avail yourself of it. When the time comes to use them, do so without panic. Potentially fatal accidents can and have occurred. The chance of starting a fire exists. Always set off flares away from tanks, gas bottles, engines, etc.

5. In a pinch, a metal bucket of flaming rags, a fired gun or a signal mirror can work. Obviously, the burning materials must be used with extreme caution, and are not advised aboard GRP boats. A signal mirror, even if torn from the head's bulkhead, can, providing the weather cooperates, be extremely effective. It is seen from the bridge of a large ship with greater ease than dye markers or other daytime visual signals.

6. *Important*: all signals must be used cautiously, calmly and with a regard for the realities of the seas. If you can, whatever the manner, get safely to port, do so on your own. The cost to others should be considered before haphazardly requesting assistance.

STEERING

❶ WHEEL LOCKS.

❷ HELM HAS NO EFFECT ON RUDDER.

❸ STEERING HAS LOOSE AND SLOPPY FEEL.

1. A wheel will lock if some obstruction or flotsam jams the rudder. Likewise, the same effect can occur if any of the linkages in the steering system become jammed–whether they are cables, rods or gears. Since the vessel will become all but uncontrollable should this occur, stop the vessel immediately. If inshore, anchor; if offshore, either set a drogue or allow the vessel to drift, providing the weather is settled. First check to see if any internal mechanical problems prevent the wheel from turning. If all checks out, someone will have to go over the side (see DIVING) to make repairs.

2. If the wheel has no effect on the rudder, some mechanical link has gone by the boards. In cable and quadrant systems, this is usually caused by a broken cable. Wire-rope clips can be effective in making repairs, providing the cable thus reconnected does not have to pass through a sheave. If a new cable must be installed, and none is aboard of appropriate guage and length, see JURY RIGS: RUDDERS. In a rod system, the problem will most likely be a bent linkage clamp. This may be unrepairable at sea. In a hydraulic system, the lack of response will be due to a leaking hydraulic cylinder, lack of hydraulic fluid or a split hose. Repairs depend on your spares at hand.

3. Looseness is invariably due to slack cables or a loose crank arm (in a rod-controlled system). Taking up slack or making sure all connections are tight will usually solve the problem. Looseness in a hydraulic system will usually be caused by a loose hose connection or a leaking hose or fitting. The entire system may have to be bled after repair. Follow manufacturer's instructions.

4. All wheel-steering boats should have provision for access to the rudder head and an emergency tiller designed to be *easily* fitted so that the ship can be controlled and conned from a readily accessible position.

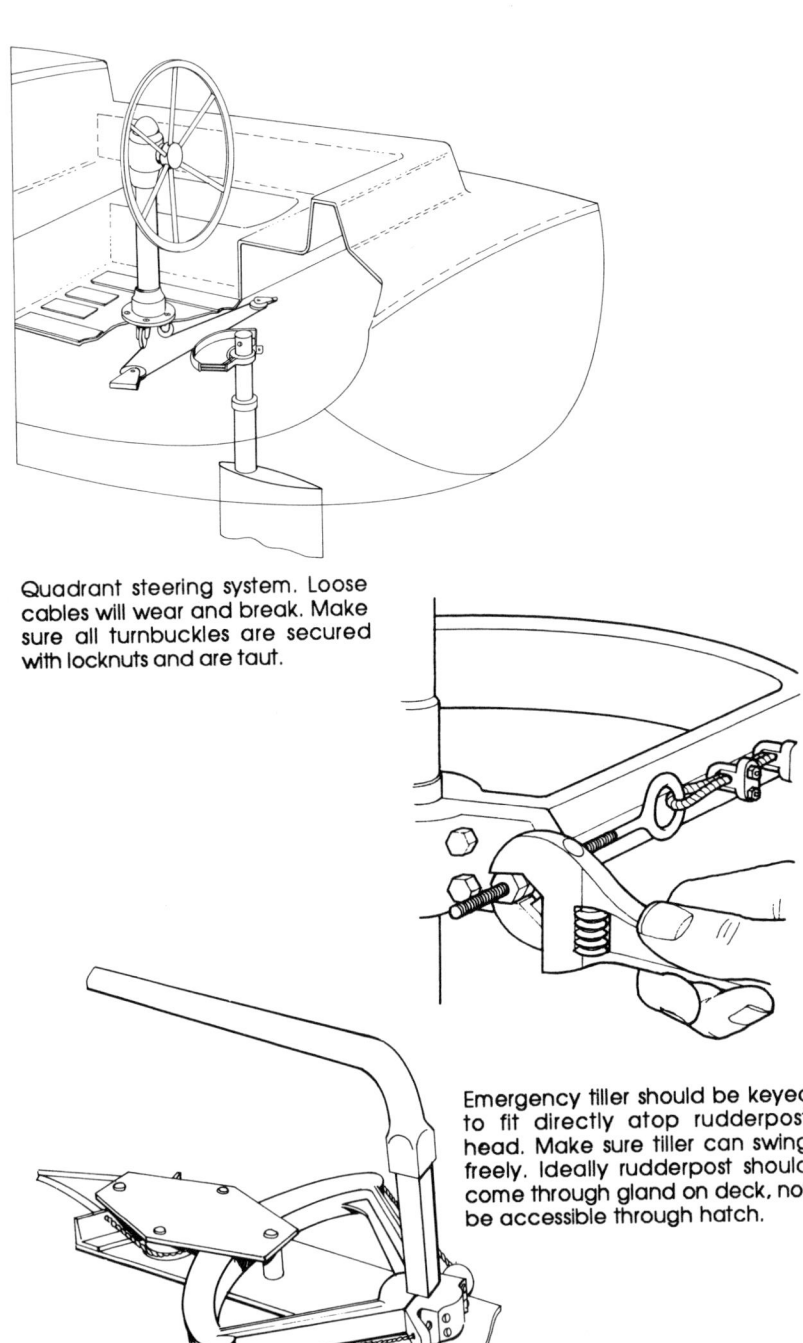

Quadrant steering system. Loose cables will wear and break. Make sure all turnbuckles are secured with locknuts and are taut.

Emergency tiller should be keyed to fit directly atop rudderpost head. Make sure tiller can swing freely. Ideally rudderpost should come through gland on deck, not be accessible through hatch.

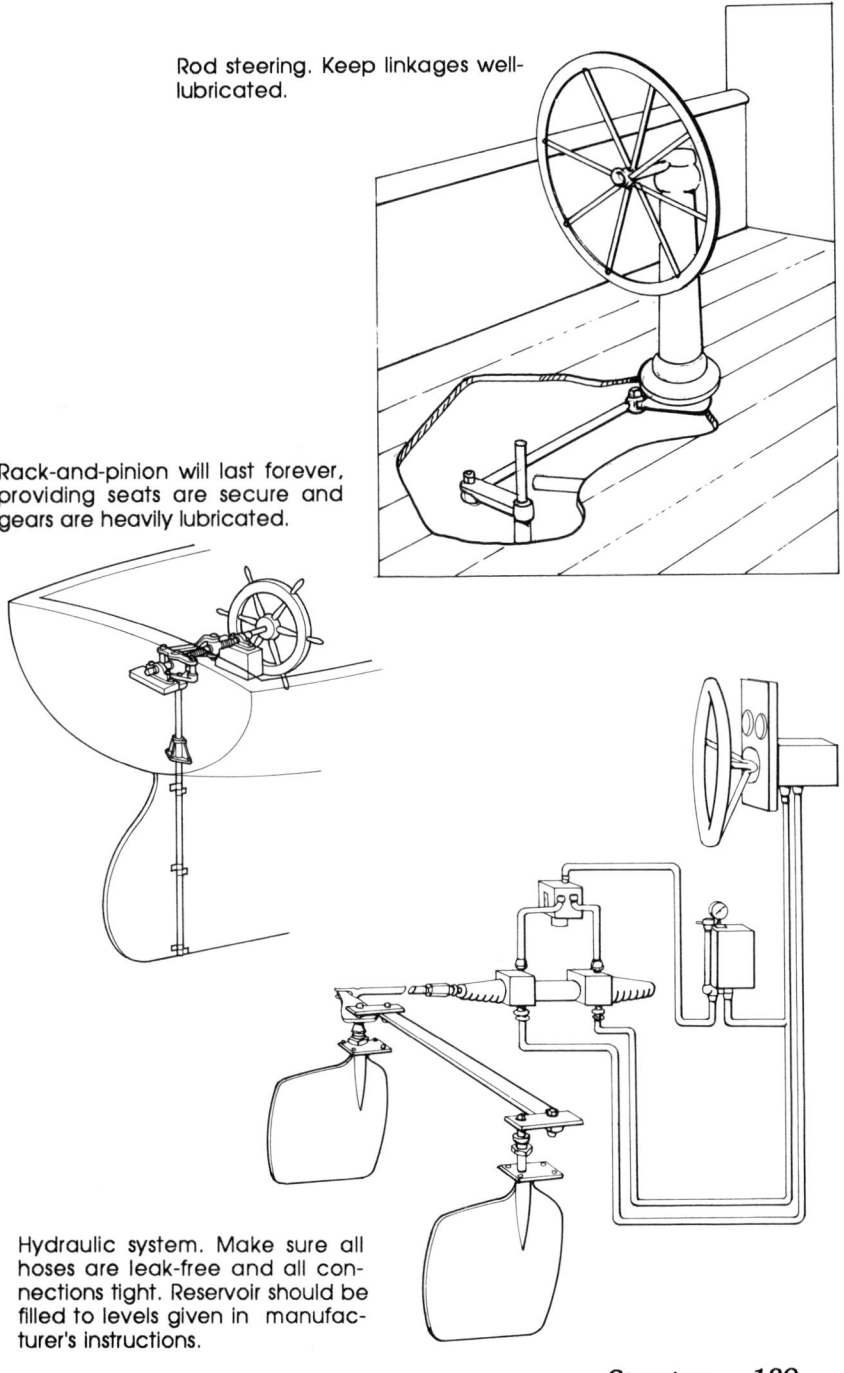

Rod steering. Keep linkages well-lubricated.

Rack-and-pinion will last forever, providing seats are secure and gears are heavily lubricated.

Hydraulic system. Make sure all hoses are leak-free and all connections tight. Reservoir should be filled to levels given in manufacturer's instructions.

TILLER: *Breakage*

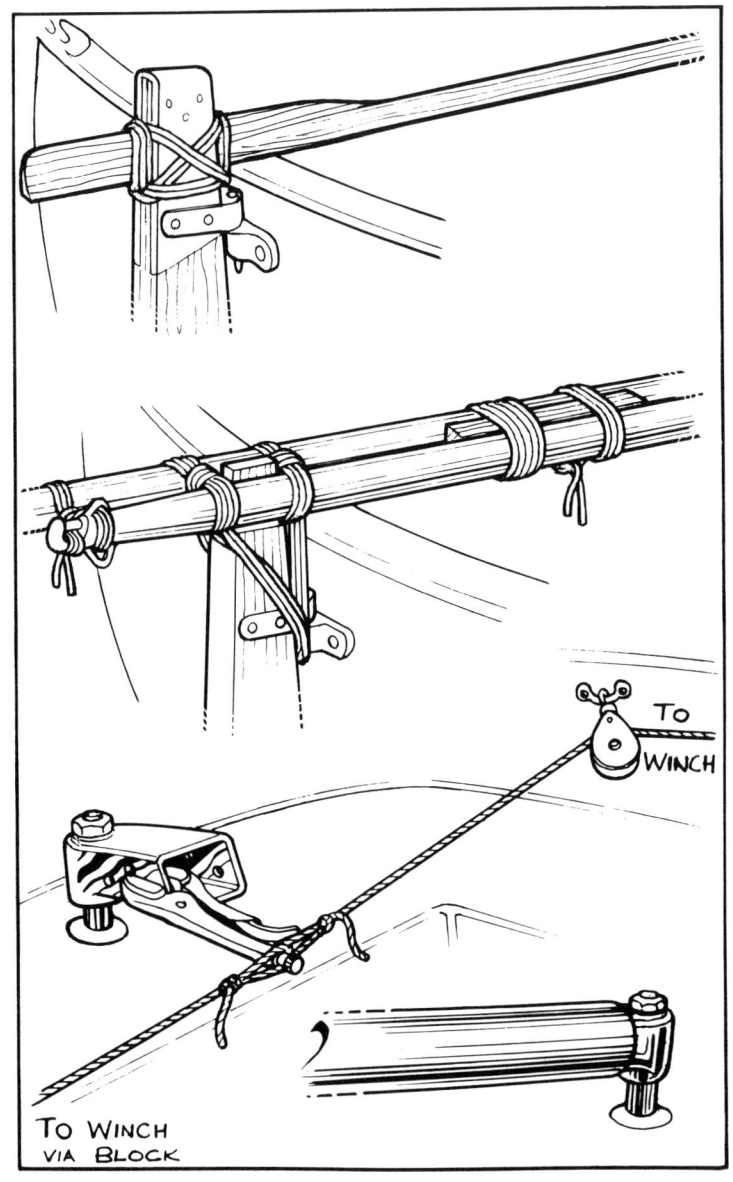

To Winch

Winch

To Winch
via Block

❶ OUTBOARD RUDDER: JAM A SECTION OF BOATHOOK OR AN OAR BETWEEN THE RUDDER CHEEKS AND LASH IN PLACE.

❷ OUTBOARD RUDDER: IF TILLER FITS TO EITHER SIDE OF RUDDER BLADE, LASH POLES OR SCRAP WOOD AROUND BLADE TOP.

❸ INBOARD RUDDER: CHEEK-TYPE FITTING, AS SUGGESTED ABOVE.

❹ INBOARD RUDDER: SOCKET FITTING, OPENING MAY NOT BE CLEARABLE. USE VISEGRIP/MOLEGRIP PLIERS WITH LINES LED TO COAMING BLOCKS AND THENCE TO WINCHES.

1. Cheeks at rudder head may also be damaged. Scrap plywood can be used as reinforecment on either side, lashed temporarily. Later, when time permits, drill three staggered holes through ply and rudder cheeks and throughbolt. Makeshift tiller can still be sashed between the new cheeks or else drilled and then throughbolted, making for a stronger, more responsive jury tiller.

2. If nothing else is at hand, use two long fiddles, such as are often found to keep settee cushions in place. These are usually fastened with self-tapping screws and can easily be refitted later; they make an elegant, either-side-of-the-rudder-head tiller.

3. Cheek fittings are usually bronze or stainless steel and the wood may have swelled between them, the tiller having broken slightly above the fitting. Knock out retaining bolt and swelled wood fragments. This will require a chisel and mallet. The same tools can be used to shape the wood replacement. Remember, any jury tiller will be weaker and offer a less than ideal position for maximum leverage.

TOWING

❶ IF YOU ARE THE VESSEL TO BE TOWED:
    1. DROP SAILS AND SECURE.
    2. POSITION ONE CREW MEMBER AT THE HELM.
    3. SECURE BITTER END OF HAWSER TO STRONG POINT ON DECK (SEE BELOW).
    4. WHEN TOWING BOAT APPROACHES FROM LEEWARD SIDE. HEAVE HAWSER TO HER WAITING CREW.
    5. INSTRUCT TOWING VESSEL AS TO YOUR MAXIMUM SPEED

AND ALLOW HER TO PROCEED, STATIONING A CREW MEMBER FORWARD TO PASS SIGNALS.

❷ IF YOU ARE TOWING A VESSEL:
 1. APPROACH THE VESSEL TO BE TOWED FROM HER LEE-WARD SIDE.
 2. WHEN CROSSING HER BOWS, EITHER PASS OR ACCEPT TOWING HAWSER.
 3. TRY TO FASTEN THE TOWLINE TO STRONG POINTS FOR-WARD OF THE RUDDERPOST TO AID IN MANEUVERABILITY.
 4. PROCEED AHEAD SLOWLY, HANDING OUT THE TOWLINE UNTIL TAUT.
 5. POSITION ONE CREW MEMBER AFT TO SEE THAT LINE RE-MAINS TAUT (TO AVOID FOULING YOUR PROP) AND TO ACCEPT HAND SIGNALS FROM THE DISABLED BOAT.

❸ TOWING UNDER SAIL:
 1. PASS THE DISABLED VESSEL'S BOWS FROM LEEWARD.
 2. HEAVE TOWLINE AS YOU PASS HER BOWS.
 3. HEAD OFF ON A REACH OR RUN.

1. Dropping sail is obviously not applicable in a powerboat. How-ever, if there is a sea running, a very small steadying sail aft may make steering easier for the towed boat and maneuverability greater for the towboat.

2. Crew should be positioned at the helm, forward and at standby. All must be ready for immediate action, especially as might concern recovery of the towline.

3. Many contemporary boats do not have adequate foredeck cleats. A towing hawser handed by a commercial vessel will be quite large, and even if the cleats were enormous, very likely they would only be through-bolted to a backing pad. Decks have been ripped up. The ideal foredeck attachment point will be a samson post properly locked into the keel or stem. Lacking this, it is perhaps best to secure the towline around the base of the mast, or, on a powerboat, around the entire house. Alternatively, the towline can be attached to a bridle led around either side of the house to the cockpit winches and then cleated. In any case, it is a good idea to bend a piece of (comparatively) light stuff to the hawser and tie its bitter end to a deck cleat; the bend to the hawser should be for-ward of the stemhead. In case the towline slips or chafes through at the stem, this "safety" line will make it that much easier to re-trieve it.

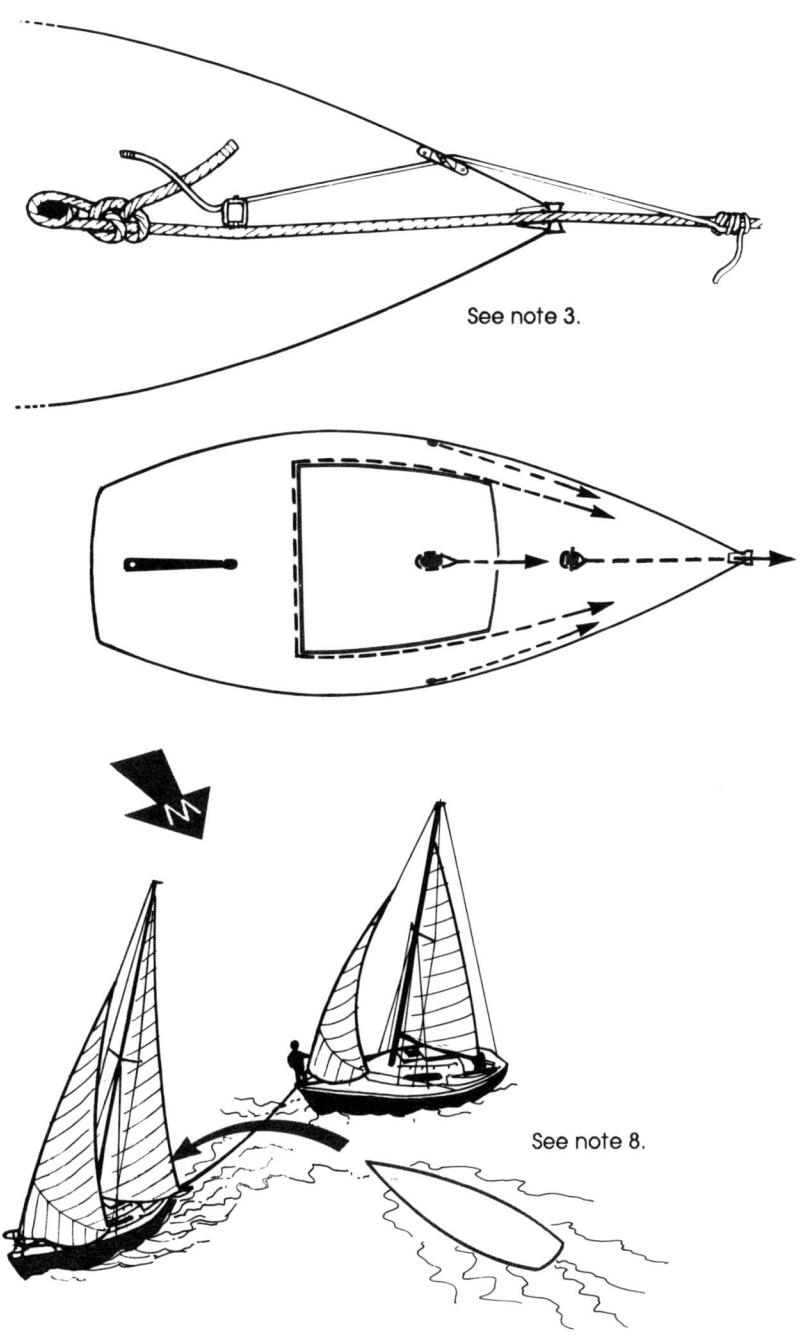

See note 3.

See note 8.

4. Always approach from the leeward side of the disabled vessel. You will then be able to avoid either drifting down on the vessel or overshooting it. Whether you should accept a towline or pass over your own is not a clear point of maritime law, see SALVAGE.

5. All tows must be undertaken at slow rates of speed. Quite often, commercial ship operators do not fully understand the limits that can be imposed safely upon a yacht under tow. What happens is either the towrope snaps or your foredeck has a good chance of disintegrating.

6. Hand signals are the only way to communicate properly during a tow. These must be arranged prior to the actual commencement of towing, and crew should be stationed on both vessels expressly for the purpose of signaling.

7. If you are the towing vessel, a bridle, carrying the towrope to either quarter or to the winches, will enable you to maintan a straighter tow and allow for more fluid handling, as well as keeping the rope clear of the propeller. It will prevent your vessel from skewing from side to side and will better distribute the towing strains.

8. Under sail, tows can be very efficient. They also allow for better communication between vessels, and more precise handling, believe it or not. Since the sails can be trimmed to help steer the boat, there will be less strain on the rudder assembly. Also, there will be little chance of dragging the disabled vessel at imprudent speeds.

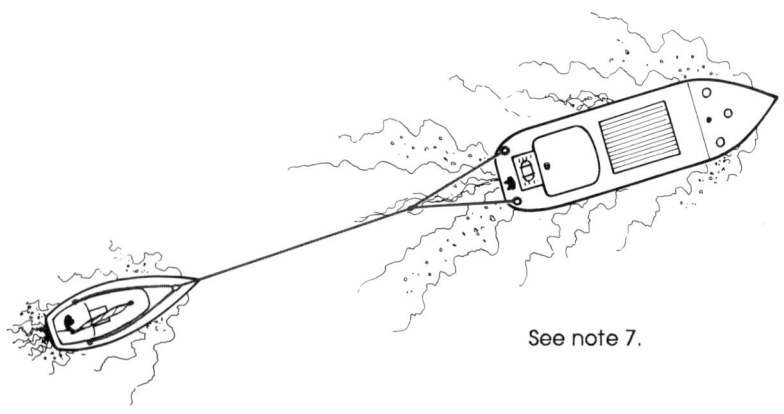

See note 7.

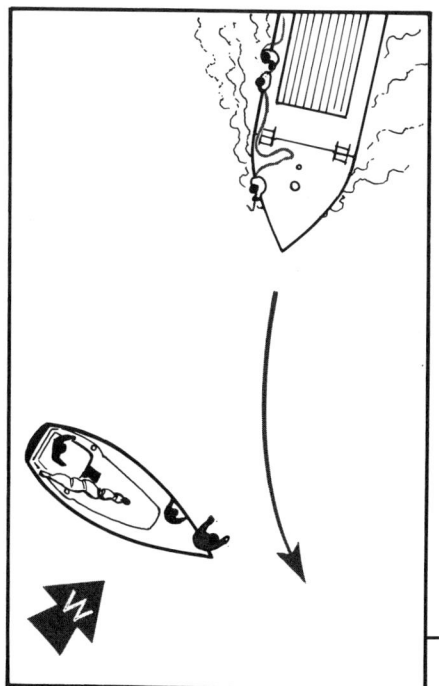

See note 4.

See note 6.

Towing   *145*

WATER

❶ TO OBTAIN, USE RAINWATER, DISTILLATION.

❷ TO PURIFY, USE BLEACH OR IODINE.

1. Rainwater can be caught in awnings, buckets, from the mainsail, etc. Allow it to run for a few minutes to rinse off any salt adhering to the catchment. Distillation can be carried out using a large pot on the stove with a funnel-like cover secured over it. A tube should run up and over, then down to another container. Wrap the central portion of the tube with rags. As the water boils, pour cold seawater on the rags; this will condense the steam in the tube and leave the crystalized salt in the pot, producing reasonably salt-free water.

2. Household bleach can be used to purify and make palatable drinking water that may be tainted or old. Use 2 drops per quart or litre of clear water, double if the water is cloudy. Iodine (2%) can be used instead in the ration of 5 drops per quart or litre of clear water, double if the water is cloudy. Let stand for an hour before using and aerate by pouring back and forth between containers.

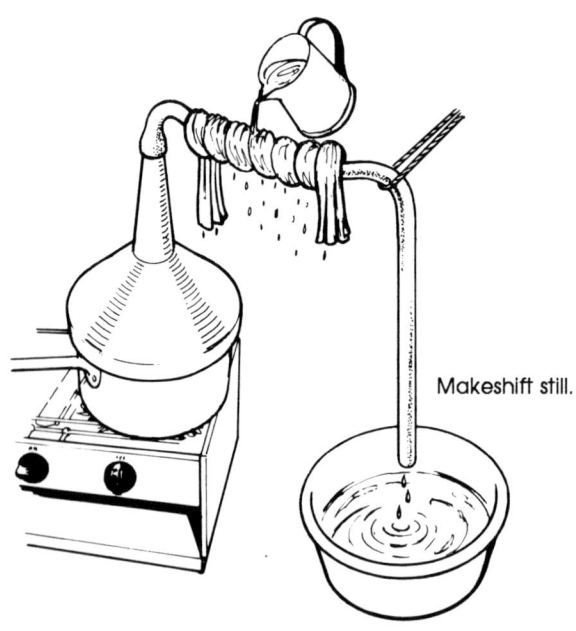

Makeshift still.

REPAIR KIT

Everything for repairs, painting, spares and emergencies collectively can be included in the bosun's locker. One should plan this equipment with reference to the size of the boat, stowage space aboard, type of voyaging expected and cost. Obviously, if you are planning a voyage to the South Seas of three years' duration, what you must plan for and carry with you is likely to be vastly more and different than if you take a two-week coastal cruise every summer. Many seamen stock up on everything, at great cost and with little forethought, without taking into account what it's all for!

The need for specific items depends on your boat's construction, size, engine, rig and type. A large powerboat will not need spare shrouds for a long passage, obviously, but it will pay to take a spare propeller and shaft, especially in out-of-the-way spots. Also, one would need tools or means to pull the prop with the boat careened or beached at low water. Likewise, four gallons of bottom paint make sense carried along on a year's cruise. There's no need for any paint aboard the weekend boat. Following are several lists of spares and tools to be kept aboard different-size yachts. None is to be taken as gospel, as each of us has different needs and aims.

FOR BOATS UNDER 30 FEET (9 METERS)

Tools
8" (20 cm) adjustable wrench
medium-size pliers
medium-blade screwdriver
10" (25 cm) vise grips
pocket rigging knife with spike
waterproof pouch to carry tools

Sail repair kit
scissors
sailmaker's wax
palm
seam ripper
hot knife
3 spools waxed polyester thread
assorted needles
1 roll ripstop tape
3'x3' (1x1 meter) piece of adhesive, sticky-backed Dacron/Terylene
light thread for spinnaker repair
telltale yarn
waterproof ditty bag

Spare parts
assorted stainless steel nuts, bolts, washers, sheet metal screws
bulbs for compass and running lights
winch pawls and springs
cam cleat springs
assorted cotter pins and split rings
clear, compartmented box to hold all

Miscellaneous
1 roll duct tape
tube of clear silicone seal
1 spray can penetrating oil
small can general-purpose lubricating oil
can of Teflon spray lubricant
indelible marking pen

FOR BOATS FROM 30-45 FEET (9-14 METERS)

Tools
Allen wrenches
chisels (1 cold chisel)
hand drill plus set of bits
files (8" or 20 cm mill bastard, 1 medium rattail, 1 triangular)
medium ballpeen hammer
50' (15 meters) measuring tape
nail set
oil stone
pliers (10" or 25 cm channel lock, needle nose, regular)
hacksaw with extra high-speed blades
6 assorted-size regular screwdrivers
2 Phillips screwdrivers
1 set jeweler's screwdrivers
vise grips (7" and 10" or 18 and 25 cm)
wire brush
wire cutters
work gloves
wrenches (8" and 10" or 20 and 25 cm adjustable, set of
    combination–open end and box)
toolbox

Electrical parts
spare bulbs for each light aboard
3 each spare fuses for each type aboard
assorted wire crimps

wire strippers/crimpers
flashlight (torch) batteries and bulbs
continuity tester
black electrician's tape

Engine and mechanical spares
3 cans oil for hydraulics
hydraulic hose and assorted end fittings
transmission fluid
set of engine filters
assorted grits wet/dry sandpaper
complete set of engine belts
one complete oil change
new voltage regulator for each alternator
6'x6' (2x2 meters) canvas drop cloth with grommets
length of 2x4 lumber
section of marine grade sheet plywood
assorted stainless steel hose clamps
drift punch
spare water pump impeller

Spares
assorted nuts, bolts and washers
assorted cotter pins
assorted clevis pins
assorted D-shackles
assorted snap shackles
1 spare turnbuckle with toggle
1 genoa car
winch pawls
winch pawl springs
winch roller bearings
spare winch handle

Sail repair kit
scissors
sailmaker's wax
2 palms
2 seam rippers
hot knife
light thread for spinnaker repairs
6 spools waxed polyester thread
assorted needles
ripstop tape
3'x6' (1x2 meters) piece of sticky-backed Dacron/Terylene
   yarn for telltales

25' (8 meters) stainless-steel or monel seizing wire
3 D-rings
sailmaker's pliers
ditty bag

Sealants and lubricants
2-part epoxy
2 tubes clear silicone sealant
2 cans spray penetrating oil
1 can general-purpose lubricating oil
1 can Teflon spray lubricant
2 rolls duct tape
silicone or lanolin grease
indelible ink markers
1 can anti-seizing spray

FOR YACHTS 45 FEET (14 METERS) AND LARGER

Tools
Allen wrenches (long and short)
awls (small and large)
block plane
chisels (1 cold, 2 wood)
hand drill with set of bits
variable-speed rechargeable electric drill with set of bits
files (8", 10", 12" or 20, 25, 30 cm mill bastards, 3 wood files,
    2 rattails, 1 triangular)
hammers (16-oz. or 500-gram ballpeen, baby sledge, claw, rubber
    mallet)
measures (100' or 30 meters tape, fold-up rule, calipers)
mirror (1 retrieving)
nail sets (5 assorted)
oil stone
pipe cutter
pipe, 18" or 1/2 meter (as battering ram and as Spanish windlass)
pliers (2 channel lock, 2 needle nose, 4 regular in assorted sizes)
2 putty knives (1" or 2.5 cm)
saws (crosscut, hacksaw and 40 blades, jigsaw and 12 blades)
screwdrivers (17 assorted regular, 6 assorted Phillips, 2 offset,
    1 jeweler's set)
tap and die set (sized to your needs)
tin snips
propane torch with varying tips
vise

vise grips in assorted sizes
wire brushes (steel and brass)
wire cutters
work gloves (leather palms)
wrenches (6", 8", 10" or 15, 20, 25 cm adjustables, 14" or 36 cm
    pipe wrench, strap wrench, complete 3/8" or 1 cm drive socket
    wrench set, set combination wrenches, set open-ended)
X-Acto knife and 6 blades
tool box

Electrical parts
compass-light assembly
running-light bulbs
spare bulbs for each lamp aboard
3 of each type of fuse aboard
assorted wire crimps
wire strippers-crimpers
flashlight (torch) batteries and bulbs
assorted lengths and gauges electrical wire
black electrician's tape
silicone grease
multimeter
solder
soldering gun or iron (12-volt or flame heating)
spare anemometer cups
spare wind vane
spare knotmeter transducer
storage box

Sealants and lubricants
2-part epoxy
2 tubes clear silicone sealant
2 cans spray penetrating oil
2 cans spray silicone lubricant
2 cans multipurpose lubricating oil
2 rolls duct tape
2 indelible ink markers
silicone or lanolin grease
2 cans anti-seizing spray

Sail repair kit
scissors
sailmaker's wax
2 palms
2 seam rippers

hot knife with spare tip
light thread for spinnaker repairs
8 spools waxed polyester thread
assorted needles
2 rolls ripstop tape
2 pieces 3'x6' (1x2 meters) sticky-backed Dacron/Terylene yarn for
   telltales
2 weights seizing wire (25' or 8 meters each)
3 D-rings
3 O-rings
50' (15 meters) tubular webbing
sailmaker's pliers
assorted weight sailcloth
roll 5 oz Dacron tape, 6" (15 cm) wide
spool of light stuff for flag halyards, etc.
6 awls
grommet set (stainless steel or brass)
ditty bag

Rigging parts
Nicopress (Talurit) tool (sized to halyards and shrouds, 2 preferably)
12 Nicopress (Talurit) sleeves for each size wire aboard
assorted stainless steel thimbles
assorted snap shackles
assorted D shackles
assorted stainless steel wire in 36" (1 meter) lengths
spare turnbuckles and toggles
assorted clevis pins
assorted track cars
link plate set
spare main halyard
spare jib halyard
one length stainless steel wire 2' longer than longest stay or
   shroud

Engine and mechanical spares
1 gallon (2.5 liters) oil for hydraulics
10' (3 meters) length hydraulic hose with fittings
2 cans transmission fluid
oil for engine oil change
set engine filters, gaskets
complete set engine belts
voltage regulator for each alternator
6'x6' (2x2 meters) canvas drop cloth with grommets
assorted stainless steel hose clamps
section of marine grade sheet plywood

2-3' (1 meter) lengths 2x4s
drift punch
set of injectors
grease gun with lithium grease
2 cans starting spray
keel-bolt wrench
rudder-packing wrench
spare impellers for engine pumps (4)
spare set steering cables
master links (12) for steering chain

Spares
assorted cotter pins
assorted nuts, bolts, washers
head repair kit: pump parts, diaphragms, etc.
hand pump for oil changes
high volume bilge pump mounted on board
electric drill pump with hoses
bronze wool
assorted wet/dry sandpaper
assorted crocus cloth and emery paper
spare packing for propeller and rudder glands
winch spares: pawls, pawl springs, assorted roller bearings, split
rings, toothbrush, tweezers, dental pick, extra handles

Optional
banding tool, bands, clips
spare propeller and shaft
300' (100 meters) nylon line equal to heaviest line aboard
assorted softwood plugs sized to all through hulls

Needless to say, putting everything on a small boat would
quickly lead to foundering. Nevertheless, you should have on board
all the basics needed to make those repairs which are vital to the
voyage you are undertaking. In addition to the tools and spares
above you should have other spare supplies on hand, logged in and
replaced when necessary.

Adhesives
A tube of silicone sealant, a package of 2-part underwater epoxy,
a small can of 2-part patching compound, a tube of all-purpose ce-
ment.

Rope

At least 100 feet (30 meters) of the heaviest line used aboard, spare halyard, extra dock lines, extra anchor rode (nylon), assorted small stuff for sail ties, lashings, etc.

Miscellaneous

Rigging knife, extra flashlights, spare batteries for every piece of equipment aboard, anchor light, stove fuel, spare engine oil, emergency flares, etc.

INDEX

THE AUTHOR

Tony Meisel is a writer and editor in New York. He has been deeply involved with boating for over 40 years and has cruised and raced extensively under both power and sail in U.S. waters, England and Scandinavia, the Caribbean, the Mediterranean and the Pacific. He has written for both book and magazine publication, and currently sails his sloop *Footnote* out of New Suffolk, Long Island.